Seeking the Spirit Within

Seeking the Spirit Within

Experiencing Union with God Through Breath

Shereen Yusuff

Foreword by Fr. Andreas Kramarz, LC

IMAGE
NEW YORK

Image
An imprint of the Penguin Random House Christian Publishing Group,
a division of Penguin Random House LLC

1745 Broadway, New York, NY 10019

imagecatholicbooks.com
penguinrandomhouse.com

Library of Congress Cataloging-in-Publication Data
Names: Yusuff, Shereen author
Title: Seeking the spirit within / Shereen Yusuff;
foreword by Fr. Andreas Kramarz, LC.
Description: First edition. | Broadway, New York, NY: Image, an imprint of the Penguin Random House Christian Publishing Group, a division of Penguin Random House LLC, [2026] | Includes bibliographical references.
Identifiers: LCCN 2025039635 (print) | LCCN 2025039636 (ebook) |
ISBN 9798217152216 hardcover | ISBN 9798217152223 ebook
Subjects: LCSH: Spiritual life—Catholic Church | Prayer—
Catholic Church | Breathing exercises
Classification: LCC BX2350.3 .Y87 2026 (print) | LCC BX2350.3 (ebook)
LC record available at https://lccn.loc.gov/2025039635
LC ebook record available at https://lccn.loc.gov/2025039636

Printed in the United States of America

1st Printing

FIRST EDITION

The authorized representative in the EU for product safety and compliance is Penguin Random House Ireland, Morrison Chambers, 32 Nassau Street, Dublin D02 YH68, Ireland. https://eu-contact.penguin.ie

Book Team: Editor: Matthew Burdette • Production editor: Helen Macdonald • Managing editor: Julia Wallace • Production manager: Erin Korenko • Copy editor: Rose Decaen • Proofreaders: Drew Goter, Jean Bloom

For details on special quantity discounts for bulk purchases, contact specialmarketscms@penguinrandomhouse.com.

To the Bread of Life,
who is my breath of life

The courage and strength that are in me
are not of me, but of Him who lives
in me—it is the Eucharist.*

—SAINT FAUSTINA KOWALSKA,
DIARY, 91

*The Eucharist is understood as the true presence of the body and blood, soul, and divinity of Christ.

Ruah[*]

When are we aware of our breath?
Is it only when we are in the presence of death?
Or when we are paying attention to our health?

When I look up at the stars and the moon,
or when I listen to my favorite tune.
When I smell beautiful flowers
or look up at incredibly tall towers.
When I notice the plume of birds
or see horses and cows in herds.
When I hear the giggle of a child
or hear roosters crowing in the wild.

When I experience God within and around me,
which leads me to break into dance gleefully.
There is not a moment that passes by me
when I do not appreciate breath for its magnificence and
glory.
For even though its presence is subtle
and delicate like a bubble,
it feels no need to call attention to itself,
for it knows its value and strength and its place in our
existence.

**Ruah* is a Hebrew word that is used to denote both "breath" and "spirit."

Every breath I take is a kiss from God,
gently reminding me of the intimacy I share with the universe,
of how beautiful everything is,
to enjoy and value it for all it is.

Whatever I inhale or take in,
I have to exhale or let go.
Not to obtain or to possess
but to admire and to be in awe.
And the sheer magic that takes place within me
when God breathes life into me.

Our breath is our life force.
Qi, Prana, Ruah.
Breath is life,
breath is happiness,
breath is love.
God is love.
May we all experience God's breath within us.

Foreword

Breathing and spirituality have rarely shared a common space in the Catholic tradition. Yes, the Holy Spirit, referred to as God's breath or "wind" (*ruah*), is mentioned in the creation narrative (Genesis 1:2) and when Christ breathed upon the apostles after His resurrection (John 20:22), but many people only pay attention to their own breath during relaxation exercises.

Thanks to Shereen Yusuff's training as a certified breath coach, her personal faith journey, and her selfless dedication to writing this book, we now possess in written form a unique way of bringing these two realities together. She converts our continuous act of breathing, one of the most basic bodily functions, into a deep spiritual experience.

Before I was graced with meeting Shereen in a course on spiritual direction at Divine Mercy University in Virginia, I had never been exposed to any intentional way of dealing with breath. At first, I was rather skeptical about the usefulness, let alone necessity, of looking into my breathing. I thought this practice was only for runners, opera singers, or divers. Why would I spend any time or effort on it? But the message in this book, together with individualized coaching, has changed my life. Not only have these exercises elicited an almost immediate improvement in some areas of bodily and mental functioning—from reducing allergic sneezing and congestion to greater alertness and emotional balance, just to mention a few—but they have also led me into previously uncharted territory in my relationship with God.

What Shereen does is make us aware of something that is so subtle, so intimate, and yet so essential to our existence. Learning to breathe better can lead to praying better and, ultimately, to loving better—loving more the way God loves. For if we experience in every inhale the love of the Creator giving us life and if we learn to listen to His loving voice in the silent rhythm of respiration, we can enter—both neurologically and spiritually—a safe space in our hearts. This space allows us to process and heal difficult, often hidden, realities, so we can enter an interior state that leads us to relate to others in a much more relaxed, emotionally balanced, and joyful way. Through the embrace of Christ's love, we are able to overcome fear and to open our hearts to others. We may then say we are on a path that leads to progress, not only spiritually but also holistically.

The heart is significant in this context. The way both holy Scripture and ordinary language use the word *heart* signifies a spiritual reality that connects all the operations in the human soul. While the heart is often associated primarily with emotions, it is also the place where we reflect (just as Mary "pondered [all the words] in her heart," Luke 2:19);* understand ("I have given you a wise and intelligent heart," 1 Kings 3:12); remember ("recall in your heart," Isaiah 46:8); hope ("in him my heart trusts," Psalm 28:7); and discern ("has determined in his own mind," 1 Corinthians 7:37). The heart is the integral and integrative center of the person,** and its bodily side is the physical heart (along with other organs), which modern neurology has discovered is extensively connected with the brain and whose relevance goes far beyond pumping blood through our veins. *Heart* in general can thus stand for the meeting point between body and soul, and we can influence it physically through our breathing.

The connection between breathing and God's loving presence in our life is not something made up by pious imagination. It unearths a deep theological truth that is backed up by Scripture, beginning with "the breath of life" that the first human being received from God (Genesis 2:7) and that has been sustaining all human life ever since. Even the provision of material goods ultimately depends

*All Bible quotations in this paragraph are Father Andreas's own translations.

**This is the way Pope Francis explained the concept of the heart in his last encyclical letter *Dilexit Nos*, para. 15, October 24, 2024, www.vatican.va/content/francesco/en/encyclicals/documents/20241024-enciclica-dilexit-nos.html.

on God, who is the first cause of all physical and chemical processes.* Exploring this truth in the fundamental reality of our breathing allows us to experience more deeply that "God has no other reason for creating than his love and goodness."** Shereen carries this reality further by connecting it climactically to the mystery of the Eucharist, where the loving union between God and the believer takes place in the most intimate bodily-spiritual way possible during our life on earth, helping us to take the bodily dimension of our existence and of our faith more seriously.

In Catholic circles, the physical reality of our lives has been explored most prominently by Saint Pope John Paul II's *Theology of the Body*. It deals primarily with the sacramentality of human love as experienced in the context of marriage and encoded in sexuality. This avenue deserves to be pursued in other areas of human life as well. Catholic Church documents have been insisting increasingly on the relevance of the *integral* formation and development of the person, of the whole and as a whole.*** Shereen's

*See the *Catechism of the Catholic Church,* 2nd ed. (Libreria Editrice Vaticana, 1997), 79, para. 301: God "at every moment, upholds and sustains [creatures] in being, enables them to act and brings them to their final end."

***Catechism of the Catholic Church,* 77, para. 293.

***See Pope Paul VI, *Populorum Progressio,* March 26, 1967, para. 14, www.vatican.va/content/paul-vi/en/encyclicals/documents/hf_p-vi_enc_26031967_populorum.html; Pope John Paul II, *Christifideles Laici,* December 30, 1988, para. 58–60, www.vatican.va/content/john-paul-ii/en/apost_exhortations/documents/hf_jp-ii_exh_30121988_christifideles-laici.html; Pope Benedict XVI, *Caritas in Veritate,* June 29, 2009, para. 15, www.vatican.va/content/benedict-xvi/en/encyclicals/documents/hf_ben-xvi_enc_20090629_caritas-in-veritate.html;

book has the potential to become a key piece of a larger vision of human development that overcomes fragmentation and compartmentalization in favor of a truly integral approach.

I can only wish this book many readers. It's hard to imagine that anyone would not benefit from it. Rather, I envision that the more people were to engage in spiritual breath work, the more significant the positive shift in our human relations would be. This includes our families, parishes, schools, friends, but most importantly, our relationship with God. For if learning to find God's Spirit in our breath can lead us to love more, love better, love deeply, and love selflessly, the impact on an authentic Christian life will be noteworthy. I hope every reader will persevere in not only reading but also practicing what is laid out here and invite others to do the same.

—Fr. Andreas Kramarz, LC, PhD, research associate at McGrath Institute for Church Life, University of Notre Dame, Indiana

Professor of Cultural Studies at Legion of Christ College of Humanities, Cheshire, Connecticut

---

Pope Francis, *Laudato Si',* May 24, 2015, para. 157, www.vatican.va/content/francesco/en/encyclicals/documents/papa-francesco_20150524_enciclica-laudato-si.html.

Preface

Our hearts are sacred.

In the image of the Sacred Heart of Jesus, golden rays come from His heart, which appears radiant and healthy, even though it has been pierced by immense amounts of pain and suffering.

The Divine Mercy image also emphasizes His heart. We pray: "O blood and water which gushed forth from the *heart* of Jesus, I trust in You."

Verses on the heart appear multiple times in the Bible. For example:

> Blessed are the pure in heart, for they will see God.
> (Matthew 5:8)

> Keep your heart with all vigilance,
> for from it flow the springs of life. (Proverbs 4:23)

The heart plays a pivotal role in seeing God and experiencing His power, mercy, and grace. We must take responsibility for it, guarding it as we would a precious diamond.

The heart is the source of our life, in a physical sense, and it is the place where God abides within us in a spiritual sense. The day our heart stops beating, our life on earth stops as well. When our heart stops beating for God, we are unable to experience God's peace. As Saint Augustine said in *Confessions,* "Our heart is restless, until it rests in you."

The condition of our heart also has an impact on how we interact with the rest of the world. Pain distracts us and limits our ability to be in the present moment. It takes a great deal of energy to stay focused when one is physically and mentally in pain. Additionally, it is common for individuals with unhealthy hearts to feel anxious and worried about the future.

Since the heart is within us, a great way to access it is through our breath. The way we inhale and exhale can directly affect the way our heart beats and its general condition.

We see the connection between the breath—or spirit—and the heart in the following Scripture passages:

> The LORD is near to the brokenhearted,
> and saves the crushed in spirit. (Psalm 34:18)

> Create in me a clean heart, O God,
> and put a new and right spirit within me.
> (Psalm 51:10)

In John 15:4, Jesus tells us to abide in Him. Only when we abide in Him can He abide in us. Abiding in the Lord can mean so many things—from receiving the Holy Eucharist to resting in Him, from reading Scripture to obeying His Word. In this book, I explore the concept of abiding in Him from the angle of resting in Him through our spirit and our heart. Every breath we take and every beat of our hearts can be for Him. If Jesus abides within us, within our hearts, is it not our responsibility to ensure that we have a beautiful home for our Lord to dwell in? And more importantly, should we not have access to this home as well?

For the remainder of this book, I encourage you to consider the literal condition of your heart and breath. Someone with a "good heart" not only signifies a person who is generous and kind but also who has great cardiovascular health and has the energy to minister to others with zeal. Just like the apostles asked Jesus to teach them how to pray, we need to be taught how to breathe. It's like picking up a pen and never learning how to write—the pen would be useless. It is the same with our breath. Most of us don't recognize how powerful our breath can be in terms of leading a healthier life through sleeping better, eating well, having a stronger immune system, improving the way we think, and enhancing the clarity of our minds. It helps us understand the sources of our anger and become more patient. Intentional breathing reduces stress, anxiety, and depression and lessens the urge to adopt addictive habits. It helps us access our hearts, physically and spiritually.

My goal with this book is to help you seek the true body and blood, soul, and divinity of Christ within you—the Eucharist within. Just as maintaining a car involves ensuring the tires have the right pressure, the radiator is filled with water, and the engine has clean oil—giving us the confidence that the car will not break down when we are traveling—we should also focus on creating a beautiful vehicle for God. By doing so, we can wait patiently for Him to take the driver's seat. The less pain and noise and the fewer distractions that come from within, which are often self-inflicted, the easier it becomes for us to access our heart and, in due time, experience the presence of the Almighty within us. Resting in Him allows healing to take place, and we emerge as recharged and radiant beings, shining His light. Surrendering to God's will becomes the way we live our lives.

So, let us immerse ourselves into learning more about our breath and our heart.

Contents

Note to the Reader

You might be thinking, *Why would I want to spend the next few weeks focusing on my breath? Especially when I have been breathing all my life. Surely, I can't be doing it wrong if I am still alive!*

Alive can be a subjective term. Do you go through life feeling as though you are becoming a better version of yourself every day? More energized than exhausted? Or do you deal with a lot of physical pain and emotional discomfort in your life? Practicing proper breathing can bring about a heightened state of awareness in all aspects of your life.

Being aware of our thoughts and feelings can greatly impact our ability to discern God's voice and presence. Expressions like "use your moral compass," "listen to your heart," and "follow your conscience" might strike a chord. The more present we are with our breath, the easier it is to access our hearts.

If you're someone who wants to hear the voice of God or experience God's presence in your life and have been confused on how to go about it, this book is for you.

My own journey with breath started in the secular realm, with a focus on the mind and the body. Eventually, I landed in the spiritual realm, as Saint Paul says in 1 Corinthians 15:46: "It is not the spiritual that is first, but the physical, and then the spiritual." This mirrors the structure of the book, with a focus on the mind and the body, or the physical, followed by the spiritual.

I grew up playing semi-professional tennis, then went on to participate in numerous ultra-endurance events like marathons, ultramarathons, and Ironman races, and, eventually, turned to top-tier mountaineering. These athletic pursuits drove me to appreciate the power of breath, but it was mountaineering that led me to focus on understanding breathing more fully, since the higher I climbed, the colder I got and the harder it was to breathe. Even though that was my initial reason for breath training, I quickly became fascinated by the impact breath made not only on my endurance and ability to withstand the cold but also on other aspects of my life. Being a science geek by nature and an engineer by education, I started studying more about the heart and its relationship with breath, the role of hormones, and how various chemicals in our bodies can affect our state of mind—including how happy or sad we feel. I also noticed that several of the ailments I had—such as acid reflux, allergies, sinusitis issues—started vanishing.

In my early thirties, I developed acne and suffered from

severe menstrual cramps. In the United States, birth control pills are commonly suggested as a treatment for both issues. However, I found that practicing breath and cold training significantly reduced my acne and alleviated my cramps. They also helped enhance my sports performance, including recovery between training sessions. I was able to do things on back-to-back days that I had never been able to do before. My mobility and movement improved. Breathing correctly and exposing myself to cold training enhanced blood circulation within my body, and it allowed me to cherish and be more present in nature. I started experiencing more happiness and peace, even in very difficult situations. My enjoyment at work increased as well. After fifteen years in engineering, I received a breath of fresh air in terms of how creative and energized I felt. I was making decisions faster and didn't need a lot of time to finish projects. I was happy with where I was.

My deep interest in breath eventually culminated in my becoming a certified breath, cold exposure, and mobility coach. Although engineering was my main career, teaching became my side passion.

Then, one day, my journey went from understanding the mind and body to having a spiritual encounter with God. Everything changed after that. My first struggle was my inability to process my experiences in engineering language. Science and faith are not supposed to go together! Or are they? Years later, I can confidently say that God was always present in my life. I unfortunately wasn't aware of His presence.

When I look back at that period in my life, at how many changes I experienced in a six-month period—my career, graduate education, religion—I felt like I was "dying to myself." It was as though my entire world were coming to an end, and I had no idea what I was being led to do next. My lifestyle, which I had engineered to perfection, was crumbling before my eyes. Despite how happy I'd been, it seemed as though I had reached the zenith. I had to change tracks to go further in my journey and experience a peace that I later came to know as God's peace—the peace that comes from doing God's will for me. God's perfect timing was not lost on me.

I remember that during those times all I had was (1) prayer; (2) the anchor of my unceasing breath, which gave me a glimpse of what it felt like to pray unceasingly; and most importantly, (3) the Eucharist. I often sought solitude to hear God's voice so He could continue to guide me, one step at a time, amid the chaos and the doubts of all the people who questioned my path and the decisions I was making. I am grateful for never having let go of these three things, since they led me to surrender to God and, eventually, allow Him to take control of my life.

Writing this book is a part of that journey too. When I first felt the Holy Spirit ask me to teach breath, combining faith and science, my level of discomfort soared through the roof. What was wrong with teaching the way I always had? Was it not good enough? Why should I change what was already working so well? Most of my apprehension came from feeling that faith was too difficult a topic to take on. How could I, an engineer, possibly think that I had the words to describe the love I had for God—or that He had for me? I was also afraid of facing the backlash from both religious and scientific communities, telling me that my work made no sense! Ultimately, the fear of hurting who was most precious to me, God, by not doing His holy will, surpassed my fear of not being accepted for this work, and that is when I sat down to write. It took me three years to finally succumb to the repetitive requests of the Holy Spirit.

While writing this book, I learned that seven in ten Catholics did not believe in the true presence of the body and blood of Christ in the Eucharist.* I was in shock! I immediately started reminiscing about my own journey of seeing the Eucharist for what it is. The first time I encountered the Eucharist in Adoration, I *knew* it was Him. The first time I consumed the Eucharist, I *knew* He was within me, and since then, I have never once doubted that He abides in me as I abide in Him. This kind of *knowing* does

*Gregory A. Smith, "Just One-Third of U.S. Catholics Agree with Their Church That Eucharist Is Body, Blood of Christ," Pew Research Center, August 5, 2019, www.pewresearch.org/short-reads/2019/08/05/transubstantiation-eucharist-u-s-catholics.

not come from science but from an actual encounter with God. I also believe that we must want to see Him and be ready to do all that it takes to encounter Him. After all, He tells us, "Everyone who searches finds" (Matthew 7:8). During all the years that I invested in understanding my body and my mind better, I didn't realize that I was seeking truth and love. Today, I can confidently say that encountering God gave me both. I did not know it then, but I was seeking Jesus, who is the way, the truth, and the life, and aligning my mind and heart, with the aid of my breath, helped in my journey.

Getting Ready

As you go through the exercises in this book, it doesn't matter how fast you complete them but rather how *often* you practice them. These exercises will also help you acquire self-discipline. Repetition is key!

Treat this book as a workbook and record your progress as you go along. Keeping a notebook handy for taking notes and tracking your progress will help motivate you to do the exercises. When it comes to breath work, it's crucial to not only understand the exercises but to also actively practice them.

Before embarking on a new journey, it's important to reflect on where you are so that you can keep track of the changes you experience. Conduct a self-examination of the current quality of your physical, mental, and spiritual well-being. Be patient with yourself. Learning breathing exercises can be as frustrating as trying to master any new skill for the first time. You might get so frustrated at not doing it "right" that you may want to end the journey soon after you begin, or you might feel tempted to rush through the book without taking the time to engage with the exercises. Both approaches will limit the amount of progress you will be able to make over the coming weeks. My advice is not to rush through the book but to follow a reasonable timeline and be honest with yourself about when you are truly ready to move forward to the next exercise. A general rule of thumb is to spend the same amount of time, perhaps a week, on each exercise before progressing to the next step. Treat this book like a Bible study, where you are expected to do one chapter a week, spending ten to fifteen minutes a day doing the exercises, if not more. There may be a step or two where you may want to spend more than a week, and that is perfectly fine. Taking things slowly is preferable to racing through each chapter. The time frame for each exercise is only a guideline. Consistency is more important than perfection.

If you're doing the exercises with a group, which is also a very effective way to implement this book, try to agree upon a set time when you will be checking in with one another, perhaps weekly. Share your victories and struggles as the weeks go by.

The most important thing to remember is that you are on the journey of building awareness around how you breathe and how your heart beats. You have been breathing and your heart has been beating all your life: You cannot fail with these exercises.

What You May Encounter Doing the Exercises

Most of the students who have done these exercises have experienced changes over a single week, while for others it has taken the entire period of ten to twelve weeks. The variation is because of each person's unique life circumstances and differing mental, physical, and physiological conditions. An athlete's physiology will be very different from that of a person who is homebound. This is also why I haven't characterized any of the exercises with what "optimal" might look like; experiencing improvement is a personal journey and can look very different for each person.

Here are a few things that may help you on your upcoming journey.

1) **Learning humility through self-knowledge**

   Here, humility is defined as being aware of what you can and cannot do—and the grace to accept this knowledge. Humility can lead to a healthy desire to change specific aspects of your life. You may notice that some of the exercises are very easy for you, while others are much harder. You will discover information in this book that is entirely new to you. Being patient with yourself as you maneuver through some of the more difficult sections in the book is key.

2) **Recognizing when you are and are not doing the exercises**

I go into a lot more detail on this topic in chapter 1, "The Fall." We sometimes prefer to pay attention only to the moments when we are doing the exercises and ignore the times when we're missing the mark. However, on the journey of breathing correctly, becoming aware of when you're not doing the exercises is just as important, since gently nudging the body to follow an intentional pattern of breathing is like teaching a child how to write the alphabet. After repeatedly doing the same act, it becomes a part of your natural way of being. You don't have to think about the act anymore and you do it without thinking. This eventually leads you to becoming aware of when you step away from what you have trained your body to do. Just as a person's handwriting can easily identify them, your breathing patterns can similarly reveal your interior state.

3) **Increasing self-discipline**

Many of the exercises require that you set aside time and do them throughout the day. Since the exercises are always structured around breath and breath never leaves us, it's easy for you to do them at any time! It's also possible to do the exercises in tandem with other activities that you might be involved in. I discuss this in more detail in the individual chapters.

4) **Building enthusiasm to continue the exercises as a result of positive changes**

Experiencing change can be powerful, leading to a domino effect that motivates you to continue the practice and also influence those around you to develop greater self-discipline and self-awareness. You might find yourself gravitating toward certain exercises over others. Even though this is natural and isn't a terrible thing, it's crucial to follow the specific exercises as they are presented each week.

5) **Finding that the exercises are becoming second nature**

After a certain point, the exercises will become part of your muscle memory, and you'll find yourself doing certain exercises even though you aren't consciously thinking about them. This is a positive sign that your body is beginning to habitually follow a different pattern from what you were accustomed to. Establishing muscle memory can take several weeks, but with intentional practice, it may start happening a lot sooner.

6) **Growing love for God, for self, and for others**

Tapping into breath brings about a more balanced way of looking at things. It frees you from whatever has prevented you from looking at yourself as being made in the image and likeness of God. The movement of your breath instigates letting go of things instead of holding on to them. You start to notice changes in your breathing patterns when you hold on to things. It also becomes easier to love and to forgive others. And once you realize that the exercises facilitate your growth in love, you'll also feel a greater desire to continue them.

7) **Discovering the ongoing nature of the journey of breath work**

Even after you finish this book, you'll find new areas of your life that you would like to bring to God—this is a lifelong process. I encourage you to always explore your *why* when you start doing the exercises, and the next section on "Conscious Self-Examination" is designed to aid you with understanding your reasons. However, along the journey, your motivations may change. If you're reading this book, something about the message or the title resonated with you, sparking a desire in your heart to explore more. Be open to this desire and keep it close. Along the way, you may gain further insights that guide you to go deeper into the root of your *why.* What matters is to be present to the ebbs and flows that you are experiencing within.

I am excited for you as you embark on this journey of self-exploration and self-awareness. Our journey with breath is designed to be gentle. The more we become aware of the subtle power of our breath, the easier it becomes to experience the subtle presence of our God at all times.

Conscious Self-Examination

In Thanksgiving for Where We Are and Where We Are Headed

Self-knowledge puts us on our knees, and it is very necessary for love. For knowledge of God gives love, and knowledge of self gives humility.

—SAINT TERESA OF CALCUTTA

Enter the room of self-knowledge first, instead of floating off to the other places. This is the path.

—SAINT TERESA OF ÁVILA

Please take this book and stand in front of a mirror, ideally one that allows you to see all the way down to your waistline.

Examine your posture as you answer the following questions:

- Do you notice your shoulders either slumping or curving in? Do you feel any tightness or pain in your neck or your shoulders?
- Turn sideways and look at yourself. Is your body slumping around the belly area?
- When you inhale, does your tummy move inward or outward? How about on your exhale?
- Do you notice a lot of upper chest movement when you breathe?
- Are you breathing through your mouth? Either on the inhale or the exhale?
- Are you breathing rapidly? Do you feel as though you are short on breath or not getting enough breath?
- Where does your tongue rest in your mouth? Up against the palate or at the base of your mouth?
- Can you hear yourself breathe?

Now take a seat and answer the next few questions:

- Are you struggling with fatigue?
- Do you have trouble falling asleep or staying asleep?
- Do you snore?
- Do you get up in the middle of the night to urinate?

- Have you been diagnosed with an autoimmune disorder like fibromyalgia or a respiratory disorder like asthma?
- Do you suffer from any mental health issues such as stress, anxiety, depression, or PTSD?
- Do you struggle with addiction? This includes pornography, drugs, alcohol, sex, and stress eating—to name a few.
- Are you struggling with weight management?
- Are you unable to make decisions?
- Are you on any medication? This includes non-prescription and pain medications.
- Do you often experience migraines?
- Do you find it hard to move on after you have experienced setbacks?
- Do you struggle with emotional management or expressing your emotions in a healthy, constructive way?

If you are a woman, please answer the following questions:

- Are you taking birth control pills to help you regulate your hormones?
- Are you taking hormonal treatment to help you with menopause?

- Do you have severe menstrual cramps?
- Are you suffering from acne? Or any other kind of skin-surface eruption?
- Are you trying to get pregnant?

If you are an athlete, please answer these questions:

- Do you find yourself short on breath while playing your sport? For example, having to bend over your knees to be able to slow down your breathing?
- Do you find yourself getting distracted by factors beyond your control, for example, crowd cheering or jeering, or bad referee calls?
- Do you find it hard to get motivated to practice every day?
- Do you find yourself not being able to recover after game day and/or not able to recover fast enough before your next game?
- Do you partake in a pre- or post-workout drink?
- Do you find yourself getting into regular arguments with your teammates, coach, and/or captain? Do you struggle with seeing eye to eye with them?
- Do you feel like quitting as soon as you start losing?
- Are you able to make decisions on the fly while being in the game?

Finally, please try to answer these questions as honestly as possible:

- Would you consider yourself a happy person?
- Are you eager to become the best version of yourself every day?
- Are you hungry to experience a deeper prayer life?
- Would you like to experience healing—physically, emotionally, and spiritually?
- Do you sit in silence? If yes, how many times a week and for how long in one session?
- Do you struggle with forgiving others and yourself?

I am confident that doing the breathing exercises shared in this book will bring about various positive changes in your life. This book is not meant to replace anything you currently utilize or practice, be it medication or prayer. Instead, it will help you explore ways to enhance your current life and relationship with God through breath.

Prayer Before We Begin Our Journey Together

Set an intention to commit to doing the breathing exercises for the next few weeks. Nothing is considered too small or too big in the realm of intentions. If you struggle to believe in the true presence of Christ in your heart or in the Eucharist, then pray for this to be revealed to you during your exercises. Every time you're aware of your breath, you are engaging in breath work and activating, subconsciously, your intention. Knowing your *why* is just as important as learning the *how.* Your *why* will be the reason for you to do your exercises every day.

I invite you to say the following prayer, which was written by Saint Augustine, as you begin your journey in walking through this program with me.

Breathe in me, O Holy Spirit, that my thoughts may all be holy.
Act in me, O Holy Spirit, that my work, too, may be holy.
Draw my heart, O Holy Spirit, that I love but what is holy.
Strengthen me, O Holy Spirit, to defend all that is holy.
Guard me, then, O Holy Spirit, that I always may be holy.

Seeking the Spirit Within

1

The Fall

Setting Yourself Up for Success

Though they fall seven times, they will rise again.

—PROVERBS 24:16

When I thought, "My foot is slipping,"
your steadfast love, O LORD, held me up.

—PSALM 94:18

Most of the time, when people refer to the Fall, they're talking about Adam, Eve, and the fruit. Whenever I think of the Fall, my mind immediately goes to Jesus falling three times before He was crucified. I love this image because knowing that Jesus fell three times on His way to the Cross makes me believe that my falls are also an important part of God's plan. My falls make my heart meek and humble, but they also inspire me to keep my gaze on every step I take to minimize unnecessary falls in the future.

I also remember that Jesus had help along the way. Through all the pushing, shoving, and kicking, Simon of Cyrene lessened Jesus's burden (Matthew 27:32). We play the roles of Jesus and Simon at different times. Sometimes it is others' burdens that we are lessening by walking alongside those who need our love and support. Sometimes we're the ones falling, carrying the heavy burden, executing God's plan, while feeling the constant shoving and pushing of others around us.

I reflect on the distance that Jesus had to traverse for Him to be crucified. Had the distance been short, He might not have met Veronica, Simon of Cyrene, or His mother—Our Lady. He would not have been able to talk to the wailing women or experience Veronica's endearing act of wiping His face, which occurred after He fell the first time. There were a lot of people whom Jesus ministered to while on His journey to fulfilling God's plan for our redemption.

Sometimes having a winding path with a lot of falls may not be bad—we get to execute God's plan by experiencing the falls and meeting our own Simons and Veronicas, creating moments of endearment. Sadly, we may encounter people who try to trample and kick us while not offering any help at all. However, the ones who do help us and love us, despite our closeness to the ground or burden of a heavy cross, really make strong impressions. These moments of love shine through a dark night like a beacon of light and inspire us to do the same for others.

Your journey with breathing exercises will be similar. There will be days when you have no desire to do the exercises, and that is perfectly fine. It is like the times when you didn't want to stick to your diet, go to bed on time, refrain from eating sugar, help the homeless person, say the Rosary,* or go to Holy Mass. The awareness of these moments is just as important as having the moment itself. Every time you have a fall, either by not doing your practices in a disciplined fashion or catching yourself breathing in a way that's not recommended in the coming pages, unite yourself with the Fall of Christ. Recognize that His falling and getting back up was a part of His divine plan, just as it may be a part of yours. You can fall a million times, provided you rise a million times. Doing my breathing exercises is like brushing my teeth—a task so essential that others would suffer if I didn't complete it. And so, if you're the kind of person who is constantly looking to do something nice for another, do your breathing exercises!

Work on yourself first before you decide to advise others to follow your ways. The best way to minister to others is not through words but through actions. It is always helpful to have others keep you accountable when you are

*The Rosary helps us meditate on the lives of Jesus and Mary. For guidance on how to pray it, this is a great resource: "How to Pray the Rosary," United States Conference of Catholic Bishops, www.usccb.org/how-to-pray-the-rosary. Another great resource is the book *The Secret of the Rosary* by Saint Louis de Montfort.

attempting to do something new. Bring your Simons and Veronicas along with you on this journey, and, who knows, they might end up doing the exercises as well; then you can all work on embodying Christ's light and experience the power of the Holy Spirit together.

Exercise

The first exercise is to become aware of how many breaths you take in a minute—which is your respiratory rate. Use a timer to count the number of inhales you take in one minute. Write down this number and keep it in your record, along with your responses from the self-examination section earlier in the book. You need to do this exercise only once this week, but you will be tracking your respiratory rate in the coming weeks.

Next, you are going to practice seeing what your body does while you are breathing. Put your hand on your stomach and observe the movement of your hand while you are breathing. You should feel a gentle outward movement on the inhale and a similar inward movement on the exhale. If you're struggling to feel this movement, you can lie on a flat surface and rest a book on your stomach. You should see a gentle rise when you inhale and a gentle fall when you exhale. Don't try to force your stomach in and out, but rather observe the natural motion of your stomach as you breathe. If you notice that the movement is the opposite of what was just described, then intentionally work on raising the book on the inhale and letting it fall on the exhale. Breathing with this intention will begin the process of retraining your body to breathe correctly. If you're unable to do this exercise, ask a friend or family member to breathe and watch their body's movement. Watching another person do the exercise correctly can teach you to do it correctly as well.

Once that is done, set an alarm for every hour on the hour. When it sounds, take at least a minute to focus on your breathing. If this is too much for you, choose times of the day when you can commit to becoming aware of your breath. I suggest coupling the exercise with something you're already doing. For example, you can do the exercise every time you step into a car or every time you are standing in line at the grocery store or waiting to get cash at an ATM. The options are limitless as to how you can incorporate this exercise into your life. *This exercise has more to do with the awareness of your breath than it does with how you are breathing.* In the upcoming chapters, we will go into the *how,* but for now, you can practice freely.

As explained previously, there will be moments or days when you completely forget to be aware of your breath, which would be considered a fall. Treat your falls with patience and love, thanking them for giving you opportunities to pick yourself up again and to keep moving forward with the exercise. The act of not being aware of your breath is just as important as being aware of your breath.

Reflection Questions

1. On a scale of 1 to 10, how hard has it been for you to be aware of your breath at set times during the day?
2. Have you been able to incorporate self-discipline to stick to your pre-decided times?
3. Have you been aware of your breath outside the times that you had set to pay attention to your breath?

If the answer to the last question is "Yes, often," then it's time to move forward.

2

Wide Gate Versus Narrow Gate

Breathing Through the Mouth and Through the Nose

The LORD God formed man from the dust of the ground, and breathed into his nostrils the breath of life; and the man became a living being.

—GENESIS 2:7

Enter through the narrow gate; for the gate is wide and the road is easy that leads to destruction, and there are many who take it.

—MATTHEW 7:13

In the previous chapter, the focus was on becoming aware of the act of breathing, for we know how easy it is to go through our days without realizing that we are breathing—just as we may not always be aware of God's presence around us and in us all the time. Now we will focus on the *how* of breathing. Our main breathing organ is the nose. Our mouth is the primary organ for eating, drinking, and speaking. It's a secondary organ for breathing and is necessary when scuba diving or snorkeling, or when we climb high mountains and the air is thin and cold. Unfortunately, most of us, at an early stage in our life, recognize the "wide gate" on our face and start breathing through the mouth because we can intake a larger volume of air more quickly.

Is this a good thing? It depends on the situation. For athletes needing quick bursts of energy during an hour-long game, taking short, deep breaths through the mouth can be advantageous. It is also helpful when facing challenging tasks. Taking a few short breaths can help us gain focus before attempting the task. However, if you're someone who breathes more often through your mouth than through your nose, then you will end up having a weak respiratory system. Our main breathing muscle in the body is the diaphragm, and mouth breathing tends to be very shallow, not giving the diaphragm the amount of movement it needs to stay strong.

Nose breathing is the easiest way to access the diaphragm consistently. The stronger your diaphragm, the better your posture will be. Your neck pains and shoulder pains from slouching will lessen. You will also reduce upper chest (neck and shoulders) movement, for the breath naturally goes deeper, engaging the diaphragm. You might notice that breathing through your nose forces you to slow down your breathing, and the tendency to take short, rapid breaths goes away. Nose breathing allows you to take longer and smoother breaths.

When you're sitting on a couch or walking around the house, aim to make breathing both in and out of your nose your default setting. If you've been breathing through your mouth often, then switching to nose breathing may increase your urge to yawn. During the next few weeks, you might want to limit the amount of air you're bringing in through your mouth by yawning with your mouth closed. You can do this by actively keeping your mouth closed while yawning or by trying to swallow as the yawn is forming. Often, this can prevent the yawn from completely developing. Another trick is to hold and pinch your nose when you feel a yawn coming on.

Breathing both in and out of the nose may be a lot harder than you think. About 61 percent of adults identify themselves as mouth breathers.* Breathing through the nose changes the temperature of the air coming into the body to help with optimal absorption of oxygen in the lungs. Another benefit is that, within our nose, we have hairs called cilia that serve as a filter for the air coming

* Sleep Review, "61% Self-Identify as Mouth Breathers," March 9, 2015, https://sleepreviewmag.com/sleep-disorders/breathing-disorders/snoring/61-self-identify-mouth-breathers.

into our bodies—similar to the filters in our central heating and cooling systems in our houses and workplaces. Our bodies are intelligently designed with a natural filtering system that helps reduce allergens and bacteria in the airway.

When we breathe through the nose, we also increase our lung volume. Athletes often measure their lung volume using a parameter known as VO_2 max, where *V* stands for "volume" and O_2 stands for "oxygen." Specifically, VO_2 max is how much oxygen your body uses during exercise. Until a couple of years ago, it was widely believed that one was born with a VO_2 max and that it was hard to change. However, this belief has been challenged by the discovery that nose-breathing techniques can effectively enhance a person's VO_2 max.

Nose breathing also changes the profile of your face. When you breathe through your nose, your nasal cavities get wider; as a result, nose breathing often brings about a more square-shaped face with prominent cheekbones and a jawline that often lessens the need for certain types of orthodontic treatment. And with nose breathing, your nose releases nitric oxide, which works as a vasodilator, enhancing the absorption of oxygen into the blood.

A lot of people breathe through their mouth because their nose is blocked, most often due to congestion. Yet the reality is that if you don't use it, you lose it. This reminds me of the parable of the talents, where the servant who was given one talent decided to bury it and ended up losing the one talent that he had because he didn't invest it (Matthew 25:14–30). Luckily for us, we have limitless opportunities to use our noses no matter how many times we fail to breathe through them. The more you breathe through your nose, the less your nose gets blocked. Later in this chapter, I share an exercise you can do to unblock your nose naturally instead of using nasal sprays.

When you exert a lot of effort, such as by walking briskly, hiking, or transitioning to higher altitudes, it may be important to breathe through your mouth since you'll need more energy over shorter durations. Mouth breathing has its place but should be used sparingly and only when needed. The way to gauge whether you need to mouth breathe would be to start breathing through only your nose as you begin exercising. If it gets too hard to continue, breathe in through your nose and out through your mouth. If that doesn't give you the amount of air you need, go ahead and breathe in and out of your mouth. If you catch yourself breathing through your mouth even when you are sitting and watching TV, looking at your cellphone, or reading a book, you may consider taping your mouth shut to help you break this habit.

Another way to break the habit is through the placement of your tongue. If you say the letter *N*, you'll notice that your tongue naturally rests on the upper part of your mouth, the palate. Keep your tongue in this position. The tongue is extremely strong, and having the tongue rest on your palate prevents you from breathing through your mouth and helps create wider nasal passages to bring in air through the nose. You may notice as well that your facial muscles tend to relax when you have your tongue resting at the top of your mouth.

Nose breathing can be practiced at night as well. An easy way to do this would be to tape your mouth before you go to sleep. If you wake up in the morning to find the tape still on your mouth, this will confirm that you are indeed breathing through your nose even when you're asleep.

Exercise

Maintain your focus on your breathing as you did in the previous exercise, but this time, ensure that you're breathing only through your nose while doing it, with your tongue placed on the palate of your mouth.

If you already tend to breathe through your nose, either increase the number of repetitions that you're doing during the day or start noticing the way you are breathing when listening to others during conversations at home, work, or school. Ensure that you're breathing only through your nose when watching TV, reading emails, listening to music, or washing dishes. At this stage, don't attempt to combine such breathing with significant movement. Slow walking is fine. However, anything brisker might leave you breathless or make your heart race.

If you're struggling with a blocked nose, or if you tend to wake up with a blocked nose, try this simple exercise: Take a few (4 or 5) light breaths, and on the last exhale, without completely emptying your lungs, pinch your nose shut, then vigorously shake your head from side to side. Do this movement until you're unable to hold your breath. Then release your fingers from your nose. Continue to take a few more light breaths only through your nose before you repeat the exercise on your exhale. You should experience a difference after doing this cycle about ten to twelve times. Repeat the steps till you have completely opened your nose. If you feel the urge to blow your nose during this exercise, please do so. Also, if shaking your head from side to side is not an option, you can also walk briskly while keeping your nose pinched. Stop walking while taking your light breaths through your nose. Try not to breathe through your mouth at all during the entire exercise.

Once you have unblocked your nose, continue to breathe only through your nose. The more you use your nose, the less blocked it will be.

Reflection Questions

1. Have you noticed any change in your chest and upper body movement when you breathe through your nose?

2. During the day, are you more frequently becoming aware of your breathing, even without the need to set an alarm?

3. If you're someone who gets up in the middle of the night to go to the bathroom—provided you're not drinking a lot of water for at least two to three hours before bedtime—have you noticed any difference? (Note: Keeping your mouth closed at night tends to reduce this urge.)

4. Has there been any difference in the amount you snore? (If you're comfortable breathing through your nose during the day and feel at ease doing so for prolonged periods of time, you can try taping your mouth at night to reduce snoring, as long as you don't have a condition like sleep apnea. Experiment with different tapes and amounts to keep your mouth shut. If you wake up without the tape, increase the amount used.)

5. On a scale of 1 to 10, how difficult has it been to leave your tongue up on your palate? Have you no-

ticed that it is easier to breathe through your nose when your tongue is placed there?

If you find yourself unconsciously placing your tongue on the palate without reminding yourself to do so, it's time to move to the next exercise.

3

Silent Night, Holy Night*

Silent and Relaxed Breathing

The fruit of silence is prayer; the fruit of prayer is faith; the fruit of faith is love; the fruit of love is service; the fruit of service is peace.

—SAINT TERESA OF CALCUTTA

After the earthquake a fire, but the LORD *was not in the fire; and after the fire a sound of sheer silence.*

—1 KINGS 19:12

Many people believe that to experience silence, you have to be in a quiet place. However, silence can also be a state of being where you experi-

*This chapter is titled from the hymn of the same name. See "Silent Night, Holy Night," https://hymnary.org/text/silent_night_holy_night_all_is_calm_all.

ence the flow of God's mercy through you. Just as in the silence of Christmas Eve, God's salvation was born in Jesus through Mary, so every moment of silence can be another opportunity to cultivate holy space within us in which His grace can touch us anew.

The first step to experiencing silence in your daily life is by checking to see if you can hear yourself breathe. If you can, what would it take for you not to make any sound? If you said, "Slow it down!" you answered correctly. Faster breathing leads to sound as well. Think of the amount of sound a waterfall makes compared to a meandering stream of water. Ideally, when you're not engaging in strenuous activities, the flow of air going into your nose should sound like a meandering stream instead of a waterfall.

There is a direct correlation between your respiratory rate and your heart rate. When you're sitting down, both rates should slow down. When you run, your breath rate and your heart rate should rise. The average resting heart rate is between 60 and 90 beats per minute. If you're an athlete, the resting heart rate can be around the lower 50s or high 40s. A lower resting heart rate usually implies that you have a healthy and efficient heart, provided you have a strong fitness routine.

I always believed that my resting heart rate was low because of all the sports I played; however, the more I learned about breath, the more I realized that it was the way I breathed during sports that made all the difference. To prove this, I stopped most major sporting activities for a year and focused on doing my breathing exercises. After a year, my resting heart rate had fallen even lower than it had been the previous year with all my athletic activities.

The next set of exercises will require effort for you to slow down your breath so that you don't hear any sound at all. This will help you become more aware of your breathing by focusing on the amount of sound you make.

Exercise

Continue with the exercises from weeks 1 and 2, but this time, ensure that you can't hear yourself breathe while doing them.

As you get better at being observant of the sound, start noticing the amount of sound you make in your daily activities. Then see if it's possible to reduce the sound by slowing down your breathing. When you're sitting still, there should be no sound at all.

In addition to these exercises, increase your awareness of how your feelings and emotions affect how you breathe. It's not necessary to do anything about it right now. Noticing the way your breathing pattern changes when your mood changes is all that is necessary at this stage.

Reflection Questions

1. How hard has it been for you not to make any sound at all while breathing?
2. Have you been able to change the way you breathe to reduce the amount of sound you are making?
3. Have you noticed any relation between how you breathe and how you feel? How did it change? If you experience anxiety, have you noticed any change in your anxiety and stress levels?
4. Are you now able to do more activities while making no sound with your breathing?

If you find yourself not making any sound at all most of the time while doing activities like watching TV, reading email or a book, driving, or cooking, it's time to move on to the next exercise.

4

Put Out into the Deep*

Breathing Deep and with Intention

Can you find out the deep things of God?
Can you find out the limit of the Almighty?

—JOB 11:7

Out of the depths I cry to you, O LORD.

—PSALM 130:1

When we think of a deep breath, we often picture a person taking a large breath in through the mouth, making a lot of sound both on the inhale and the exhale, and experiencing a lot of body movement.

Instead, I encourage you to think about taking a deep

*This chapter title is taken from Luke 5:4.

breath in a different way. We don't have to take in a lot of air through the mouth or make a lot of sound. Body movement can be minimal, with a focus on multidirectional expansion within the torso, expanding the back and the sides of the torso, with a reasonable movement of the tummy and the chest. The easiest way to visualize this is to imagine that your torso expands like a balloon, and you can feel the back expand into the chair that you're sitting on.

During a deep breath, let the air go deeper into your lungs instead of trying to take in a large volume of air through your mouth that gets caught in your chest. Just as Jesus asked Simon Peter to "put out into the deep" with his fishing nets to receive a full catch (Luke 5:4), you can similarly experience a full breath by using your diaphragm and feeling the expansion at your lower ribs when you inhale. Try to make sure that the shoulders remain relaxed while minimizing upper chest movement. Slow down your breath so that you continue not to make any sound. Breathing this way can be a little arduous in the beginning because it requires a lot of focus. However, over time, it will become second nature to you.

Do not underestimate the power of practicing your breathing exercises with others. Putting your hand on a friend's back so that they can feel their back expanding as they breathe can cultivate a deeper connection of love and friendship between the two of you. Breathing together puts you in resonance with each other.

Friends and family who breathe together stay together and pray together! Before you know it, you all will be walking through your darkest nights as beacons of light to one another.

Exercise

Stand in front of a mirror and watch yourself breathe. It's important to not only observe your chest and your stomach but also other parts of your body, such as your back, which might be easier to feel if your back is against something hard like a wall or the back of a chair. Also, if you place your hands on the sides of your lower ribs, you should be able to feel lateral expansion and contraction in this area. It might be difficult to feel all the parts of your torso move at the same time, so it's beneficial to focus on each body part individually before concentrating on the movement of your back and lower ribs together. Reduce your upper chest vertical movement as much as you can.

If you have a partner, ask your partner to place their hands on different parts of your back, namely the upper, middle, and lower back, as well as the sides of your ribs. Feel the expansion there as well. Having the hands of a partner on your back can really help you become aware of the three-dimensional nature of breathing.

Mobility exercises for the neck, torso, and shoulders

can help to loosen and enhance your awareness of these areas. Here are a few exercises that may help.

Neck Mobility

Turn your head from side to side while keeping your eyes in line with your shoulders. Next, look down at your shoulders as you turn your head from side to side. You will notice a difference in the way your neck stretches. And then look up toward the ceiling as you turn your head from side to side. Now synchronize the movement with your breath. For example, when you turn your head left, you inhale, and when you turn your head right, you exhale. You can experiment with this by doing one whole movement from right to left with an inhale followed by another full movement with an exhale. There is no set pattern that you need to follow. Try doing the movement in unison with your breath. Then return to your starting position. Do the cycle a few times.

Now move your head forward, while not raising it up, then bring it all the way back without tilting your head down. Keep your chin parallel to the ground. Try not to force the head to move beyond its comfortable range of motion. Do not move any other part of your body, especially your chest. When you're comfortable with the movement, combine it with breath. You can breathe in while moving your head forward and breathe out while moving your head back. After a few cycles this way, switch the breathing pattern: Breathe out when you move your head forward and breathe in when you pull your head back.

Torso Mobility

Upper back bend. Stretch both arms back, in either direction, to the sides, as if you are taking a big yawn, and bend your upper back slightly. Look up and relax your neck as much as possible while you're doing this stretch to feel the squeeze in the middle of your upper back. Inhale as you stretch back and stay here for a few seconds, holding your breath at the top, and then exhale as you relax and go back to your starting position. Do the whole cycle a few times. The focus of this exercise is to enhance mobility. It's okay not to breathe silently during the course of the exercise and instead pay more attention to matching the movement with your breath.

Standing or sitting side bends. Stretch to the side by reaching your arm straight up, then over your head to feel the stretch in your rib area. If you first bend toward your left side, reach your right hand over your head to feel the stretch in the rib area. Stay there for a few seconds, breathing in and out, feeling the side of your ribs expand. Return to the starting position by sitting or standing straight, and then switch to the other side. Do the whole cycle a few times. If you're standing, make sure to keep your feet planted on the ground and keep your knees relaxed. You may also look up to feel an added stretch in the rib area.

Shoulder Mobility

Shoulder rotation. Rotate your shoulder by moving your arm in circles from front to back and then from back to front in a controlled fashion while keeping the rest of your body as still as possible. Inhale when you raise your arm up and exhale on the way down, and then bring your arm back up in the reverse direction on the inhale and exhale on the way down. Do this for both shoulders, feeling only the shoulder joint move without moving your upper body much. To do this, you'll notice that you have to rotate your palm outward till your thumb faces backward when you do the rotation from front to back. This might require you to make smaller circles due to limited mobility in your shoulders, and this is perfectly fine. Do not force yourself to make an exact circle; rather, stay within a range that does not cause any pain. Over time, your circular range will increase.

Shoulder shrugs. Bring the shoulders up while keeping your hands by your thighs and inhaling, as if you were trying to reach for your ears with your shoulders. Keep them up for a second and then drop your shoulders sharply while exhaling. Once you have done this a few times, start doing shoulder shrug rotations by rotating your shoulders back and forth and bringing them up to your ears. Combine the movement with your breath.

Continue similar exercises with other parts of the body as well. By bringing awareness to any part of your body, you can increase the blood flow to that area. Combining the movement with your breath may help you release the tightness within the joint you're moving. You can even try to do circular motions with your fingers individually, focusing on each one of them while keeping all the other fingers still.

Continue to practice the mobility exercises at least once a day, along with conscious deep breathing as often as you can throughout the day.

You may also start implementing intentional breathing when you engage in activities that involve repetition, like lifting weights or resistance exercises. For example, if you're doing a push-up, you may inhale on the way down and exhale on the way up. You may inhale while pulling on a door and exhale while pushing a door. You can associate almost all repetitive movements with a breathing pattern that matches the movement.

Do the breathing exercises only when you can control the pace of the exercise. If you're unable to control the pace, then continue to breathe in a way that comes naturally to you and resume working on the exercise when the pace can be controlled. At this stage, you can breathe in and out of your mouth if the situation calls for it.

If you're up for a challenge, try becoming aware of the way you breathe while you walk. Start by breathing only through your nose. As discussed earlier, feel the breath going into the sides of your ribs, feel the lateral expansion, work on relaxing your shoulders, and place your tongue on the palate right behind your teeth by saying the letter *N*. This might sound easy on paper. However, when you start noticing how you breathe when you move, the task can be quite challenging. Remember to be patient with yourself. Becoming aware of how you breathe while you walk can be very frustrating initially. Over time, it becomes second nature and doesn't seem as daunting anymore.

A great way to do this would be by starting at home, where no one is watching you. Initially, you might walk like a robot and be extremely stiff, but it will get better. You can also start practicing walking at different paces and seeing how your breath changes with the way you change your walk. When you get comfortable walking, you can transition to running. Depending on how fast you're running, you might need to breathe through your mouth, but you can still match your breath with your steps.

This would be a good time to test your respiratory rate again and note the difference compared to when you first started. You may go back to the exercise section of chapter 1 if you can't remember how to do the exercise.

Reflection Questions

1. Were you able to feel the three-dimensional movement of breathing within your body? Was it helpful practicing with a partner?
2. Did the mobility exercises help you experience breath going into other areas of your body?
3. Were you able to do circular motions with each of your fingers in both directions while keeping all your other fingers still?
4. Has your respiratory rate changed since the first time you tested it? Are you taking fewer breaths per minute now? If you've not been able to get your respiratory rate to below 12, revisit the exercises in chapters 1 through 4 to help lower your respiratory rate.

If you can effortlessly synchronize your breath with your movements, maintain control over your joints, and keep your respiratory rate at or below 12, you are ready to proceed to the next chapter.

5

Two Sides of the Same Coin

Relationship Between the Inhale and the Exhale

Just as the body without the spirit is dead,
so faith without works is also dead.
—JAMES 2:26

God created humankind in his image,
in the image of God he created them;
male and female he created them.
—GENESIS 1:27

To understand breath, it's essential to grasp the concept of both inhaling and exhaling. You cannot have one without the other. It's like the union between husband and wife—two distinct persons forming a single entity. Another example would be the Father-Son relationship in God. Jesus said if you have seen Him, then you have seen the Father (John 14:9); in other words, they are one and yet they are each their own distinctive person. Similarly, breath is one, yet it is made up of both the inhale and the exhale. You cannot have breath without the inhale or the exhale.

The nervous system functions similarly. It oscillates between a fight-or-flight (sympathetic) state and rest-and-digest (parasympathetic) state. There is also the freeze state that falls under the parasympathetic nervous system and is activated by threat. A healthy nervous system is developed when you have a balance between fight-or-flight and rest-and-digest states. By tweaking the length of your inhale and your exhale, you can change the state of your nervous system. If you're feeling stressed, the easiest way to get out of the state of agitation is by extending the length of your exhale compared to your inhale. Similarly, if you're feeling lazy or sleepy and would like to energize yourself quickly, you can take a few short active inhales and release a few passive exhales. You may do a similar exercise when you're playing sports or hiking and notice you're feeling a bit tired or running out of breath. If you take a few large inhales in comparison to your exhales, you will immediately get an energy boost. If there's nothing specific you are trying to achieve, you can maintain a calm state of mind by making the inhale and the exhale the same length.

Scientific studies have shown that when you're in a relaxed state, having a respiratory rate of 5.5 breaths per minute allows for your heart to have good heart rate variability (HRV). HRV indicates the time interval between heartbeats. A higher HRV denotes a healthier heart. It also indicates a more adaptable heart, which makes you more resilient in tough situations.

Exercise

At this point, you should now be at a resting respiratory rate below 12. If you've not been able to achieve this, you may continue with the previous exercises till the end of the book and notice if there's a change in your respiratory rate as you get closer to the end. If you're still unable to do this, I would suggest meeting with a breath coach.

The first exercise is to inhale for 4 seconds and exhale for 4 seconds. If it's easier for you to inhale and exhale while looking at a timer, please do so. Over time, your breath will attain a rhythm and you won't need to use a timer anymore. Another way to do this exercise, especially if you're a visual learner, is to trace a sinusoidal wave in the air with your finger. Inhale on the upward curve and exhale on the downward curve.

You can also use a string of words or a sentence that is about 4 seconds long. That would make the entire cycle

8 seconds and about 7 to 8 breaths per minute. If 4 seconds is not easy for you to do, you can drop to 3 seconds, and if 4 is easy, you may increase it to 5 seconds. The idea is not to force the body but to allow for the natural movement of the breath to guide you toward finding the ideal starting breath duration.

Scripture is a great place to find such phrases, and you can even make up your own. Here are some examples of sentences that you can use in silence while focusing on the exercise at hand.

While inhaling (I), silently say: *The Lord is my shepherd.*

While exhaling (E), silently say: *There is nothing I shall want.*

(I) *Jesus, You are my savior.*

(E) *Come, be my light.*

(I) *Behold, I am the handmaiden of the Lord,*

(E) *be it done unto me according to Thy word.*

(I) *Here I am, Lord,*

(E) *I have come to do Your will.*

(I) *Lord, You are holy indeed, the font of all holiness,*

(E) *all creation rightly gives You thanks and praise.*

Remember, you want to be at ease during these exercises. When the exercises get easier, you may increase the length of the sentence to get a lower respiratory rate per minute.

You may also try box breathing: Inhale for 4 seconds,

hold your breath at the top for 4 counts, exhale for 4 counts, and then hold your breath after the exhale for 4 counts. You may continue breathing this way for as long as it takes before you notice that you are calmer than when you began. It can take anywhere from one minute to several minutes—depending on how stressed or anxious you are feeling—to experience calmness. If you were to draw this breathing pattern out as a figure, you would draw a box and hence the name box breathing. This exercise has been found to be calming. If sleep is what you are struggling with, then you can do 4-7-8 breathing, where you breathe in for 4 seconds, hold your breath for 7 seconds at the top, and then exhale for 8 seconds before you repeat the entire pattern.

Once you're comfortable with such exercises, you can start experimenting with uneven durations between your inhale and your exhale. When the exhale is longer than the inhale, you initiate a state of relaxation. To exhale longer than your inhale, you may inhale for 4 seconds and then exhale for 5 or 6 seconds. This is also great to do before going to sleep. When you extend the counts of your exhale compared to your inhale, you may notice it gets easier to fall asleep. You could also use this in moments of great distress, or when you are faced with mental and emotional challenges, since it signals the body to relax.

Here are a few examples of phrases to use with a shorter inhale and a longer exhale.

(I) *For the sake of His sorrowful passion*

(E) *have mercy on us and on the whole world.*

(I) *Pray for us, O Holy Mother of God,*

(E) *that we may be made worthy of the promises of Christ.*

(I) *Come, Holy Spirit,*

(E) *enlighten my heart, mind, and soul that I may do all things for the love of God.*

Once you're comfortable with these exercises, you can start matching your steps with your breath. For instance, you may breathe in for two steps and breathe out for two steps. Once that gets easy, you can increase the number of steps, especially on your exhale.

The key here is to manage the pace. If you walk briskly, breathing both the inhale and the exhale through your nose might be a challenge. These exercises are to be done only when you are specifically walking with the intention of doing the exercises—in other words, when you can control the pace. If you're walking at a faster pace, please don't try to breathe through only your nose, for this may be challenging at this stage.

Reflection Questions

1. What duration per inhale/exhale did you start with, and what duration did you end with for this week's

exercise? If you used words of prayer, what were they? Did using such phrases make the exercise easier?

2. Did you notice any change in how relaxed you felt when you took longer exhalations? Were you able to bring your awareness to your breath when you were lying in bed, ready to go to sleep?

3. Did you notice any change in your sleep this week?

If you can get your respiratory rate to 5.5 counts or lower without much effort when you are in a relaxed state, you're ready to go to the next chapter.

6

Finding Comfort in Discomfort

The Impact of Positive Stressors on Resilience

We also boast in our sufferings, knowing that
suffering produces endurance.

—ROMANS 5:3

He will wipe every tear from their eyes.
Death will be no more;
mourning and crying and pain will be no more.

—REVELATION 21:4

Science has shown that stress can be a positive experience leading to higher resilience, provided we can handle the amount of stress we are exposed to. Examples of positive stressors include sitting in an ice bath for two minutes to combat inflammation and reset our nervous systems, lifting weights in the gym to strengthen our muscles, running a few miles to build endurance, or walking barefoot over uneven or cold surfaces. It's important to add that all these activities must be done freely for them to be considered positive stressors. If they're forced on us, the experiences can be traumatic. Rendering the body more resilient by exposing it to positive stressors is called hormesis. We have all heard the saying "What doesn't kill us makes us stronger," yet it's not necessary to go to the extent of almost getting killed to receive this benefit. Today we know that it is not only possible to completely heal from tragic incidents such as a death or a divorce, but that one can even experience post-traumatic growth, which allows us to emerge stronger after a painful incident. This is why fights between a couple or friends are not always a bad thing if they're able to learn from the incident and come out of the argument experiencing more love and understanding for each other.

To understand how hormesis works, we must look at discomfort as an ally rather than an enemy. In the Christian sense, discomfort is often associated with acts of penance or offering sacrifices during Lent. When we make sacrifices, we're more likely to act in a compassionate, patient, and merciful way when we are exposed to negative stressors. This is because we have trained ourselves to be more tolerant of suffering. Most Catholics are familiar with the practice of *offering it up*. This can be powerful if we're able to see our feelings and emotions through Christ's eyes. However, we may also end up spiritually bypassing a painful situation by simply offering it up due to our inability to deal with the discomfort and not learn valuable lessons that could lead to lasting growth and resilience. In the upcoming chapters, we will learn how to be present to painful experiences from the past by using our breath as a modulator.

For now, we can use our breath to bear the pain associated with sitting in an ice bath for two minutes or turning the faucet to the coldest setting for about twenty seconds at the end of a shower. Experiencing the cold in the morning might be the hardest part of our day, thereby reducing the impact that negative stressors have on us for the rest of the day. Simply offering up our discomfort during a cold shower would lead us to a gritting-your-teeth approach as we wait for the shower to end. Instead, our goal is to calm our breath and recognize that feeling cold is a natural reaction without needing to fight or tolerate it. The same can happen if we take on a suck-it-up attitude, which limits the amount of growth we would receive from the stressor. However, recognizing cold as a positive stressor can help us be present to the cold, accept the discomfort, surrender to it, and experience peace by learning to breathe calmly, even during a great deal of discomfort.

Training our bodies and minds through positive stressors gives us the mental and physical strength to pick up our spiritual crosses every day and follow Jesus (Matthew 16:24). When we learn to breathe and experience our discomfort fully in situations of our own making, then our bodies and minds start becoming more resilient through experiences we don't have much control over. In a way, we are training for a stressful event in the future that we're not aware of today. The military is in training all the time. Soldiers don't start training when war is declared. It's the same with our minds and our bodies. We shouldn't start training when we receive news that a loved one has passed away, that we have cancer, or that we have lost our job. We should be training all the time so that when the traumatic event does occur, we are well prepared to take on the additional stress in our lives, be more prone to emerge from the unfortunate situation stronger, and position ourselves to experience post-traumatic growth.

Running away from pain can lead to distractions, addictions, or unhealthy habits in the short term. In the long term, it can lead to damaged relationships and an unsatisfied life. By incorporating hormetic stress into our daily lives, our bodies and minds are able to confront uncomfortable situations in real life, to not fear the unknown, and to be resilient in stressful situations.

I mentioned the cold because enduring it is one of the most challenging tasks I face daily. I used to hate the cold. Now I love it and look forward to it despite the nervousness I feel before an ice bath or a cold shower. I remind myself of the benefits of being in the cold, which include reducing inflammation, boosting my immune system, resetting my nervous system, and enhancing circulation within my body. The discomfort is extremely high during the duration of my cold exposure; however, the fruits of the experience have a long-lasting effect on my attitude toward everyone and everything for days afterward. If this is the price I pay for having a more patient, merciful, and compassionate attitude toward my brothers and sisters, then I am willing to put in the effort to receive this gift.

In Daniel 3, Shadrach, Meshach, and Abednego were thrown into a fiery furnace, heated seven times hotter than the customary temperature, as punishment for refusing to worship the golden statue that King Nebuchadnezzar had made. The furnace was so hot that it destroyed the people who threw the three young men into it. Yet in this furnace, Shadrach, Meshach, and Abednego sang the praises and hymns recounted in Daniel 3:52–90. I encourage you to take a moment and look at these verses right now. The verses make me aware of how God is in everything and in everyone, including the things and people that bring us a lot of discomfort. They also highlight how we need to bless both the light and the darkness, for we would not know one without the other. More importantly, we can bless the light and the darkness *while we are experiencing them.* It's great when we can look back with hindsight and notice the presence of God in our journey, but how much more resilient and powerful would we be if we experienced the presence of God while we were in the middle of a traumatic experience!

By exposing ourselves to hormetic stressors throughout our day, we can practice the experience of surrendering to God and blessing God during those controlled painful moments. When I go into the ice bath, I take the time to be silent in my mind; I surrender to the pain I am experiencing, fully knowing that I am safe. I focus on my breathing, quiet my restlessness, and end with prayer, blessing the Lord for all the ways He has given us to experience union with Him: "Bless the Lord, ice and cold; sing praise to him and highly exalt him forever" (Daniel 3:69). I do this in extreme heat or while I climb mountains; I praise the Lord for all His gifts, for both comfort and discomfort. The more I do this in controlled environments of my own making, the easier it becomes for me to praise the Lord even amid negative stressors that are out of my control. Over time, the negative stressors become welcome opportunities that inculcate joy and excitement versus dreaded events that I simply tolerate.

Eventually, we become like Paul and Silas, who were singing hymns and praying to God with joy even while they were locked in a prison cell (Acts 16:25). Or like the apostles who rejoiced after getting flogged for speaking in the name of Jesus (Acts 5:40–41). The joy they experienced from following God's will for them far exceeded the pain and discomfort that following God's will may sometimes bring. This joy gave them the courage to continue walking the path despite the hardships they faced.

Exercise

Cold exposure may not be a problem for some, but for most of us, it is a very scary, anxiety-inducing experience. It's important to remember that no one is forcing you to do this exercise, and you are doing it because you're aware of all the benefits that the cold can have on your body. The number of benefits I mentioned previously are only a few compared to a vast number of further benefits that the cold offers. The key is to increase your exposure over time without forcing the body to stay in the cold. Start with a goal of gradually increasing your exposure time to at least two minutes. If you want to begin by putting just your hand into a bowl full of ice water for at least a minute, that is a good start. You might enjoy splashing your face with cold water or rubbing an ice cube on the nape of your neck. Any amount of exposure is better than no exposure.

When in the cold, bring your focus back to the breath and allow for the exhalations to increase in length to prevent feeling the urge to flee from the situation. The nervous system usually takes about ninety seconds to acknowledge that you're not in danger, after which the experience becomes more bearable. Exposing yourself to the cold for at least two minutes can lead to a reduction in the amount of discomfort you experience, not only in the cold but also in other situations.

You can also incorporate the cold by turning the knob of your faucet to the coldest setting when you're finishing your shower. You may begin by facing your back to the cold water and allowing it to fall on the nape of your neck. Once again, remember to breathe in a controlled fashion, focusing on longer exhales while you are doing this exercise. Once you have allowed the water to fall over your back, you can turn around and do the same with the front of your body. Please remember the suggestions made here are only a guide. Experiment a little to understand what suits you best. Aim to get the time up to around two minutes of total cold exposure, if you can. For those who enjoy this exercise and begin to see benefits, you may, over time, allow for the cold water to fall on your face (exhale and hold if you need to while doing this) and on your head as well. Bear in mind that the number of nerve endings in the head intensifies the experience, so try not to do it at the beginning, but allow your body to get used to the cold for a bit first. At all times, be attentive to your breath while paying attention to longer exhales, and over time, you might be able to breathe normally, even during your cold showers, implementing everything you've learned so far.

You can also find other innovative ways to expose yourself to the cold, like taking a short walk without a very thick jacket on a cold day. The key to all these exercises is to have fun while doing them and never to force the body to go beyond what it can safely do. The cold is a great positive stressor; however, it must be handled cautiously. If you intend to do more extreme exercises out in the open, please ensure you're never alone while doing them. Anything beyond a small dose of cold exposure should not be attempted without first consulting a trained professional who knows how to help you in the event that you are in danger of hypothermia.

Over time, you may notice changes in your mood and levels of happiness, a stronger immune system, and a higher level of tolerance to stressful situations around you.

Reflection Questions

Give yourself about a week of exposure to the cold at the end of your shower, and then you may answer these questions:

1. How hard has it been for you to expose yourself to the cold? Has it become easier over time? How do you motivate yourself to continue with the practice?

2. Are you willing to take a full two-minute cold shower? If so, can you set a date on your calendar committing to doing this and train toward achieving that goal?

3. Have you been able to find other innovative ways to incorporate positive stressors into your life?

When you feel you can expose yourself to the cold without feeling the need to complain about it, or you find yourself thanking God for the difficult situations you're in, it's time to move forward with the exercises in the rest of this book. Be patient with yourself when it comes to the cold. This is a difficult exercise for most people, and acting with compassion and mercy toward yourself during practice is key.

7

Fasting

Intermittent Breath Fasting (IBF)

We fasted and petitioned our God for this,
and he listened to our entreaty.

—EZRA 8:23

Yet even now, says the LORD,
return to me with all your heart,
with fasting, with weeping, and with mourning.

—JOEL 2:12

Fasting with food is a well-known practice. Lent is usually the time when we actively participate in fasting and abstaining from unhealthy things we do or unhealthy foods we eat. But have you ever considered fasting from breath? Now, before you get worried, I would like to share a few data points about breathing. A healthy person can hold their breath for 25 to 45 seconds after a relaxed exhale. Certain breathing techniques can show you how to hold your breath for 1 to 3 minutes. The world record for the longest breath hold is a little over 24 minutes. Human beings have found ways to survive without feeling the need to breathe every second. It might also be worthwhile to recognize that we tend to over breathe when we struggle with anxiety or panic disorders. Another way to look at this is to remember that just because we have mouths and stomachs to eat and digest our food, we don't constantly eat. If we did, then we'd be unable to fit into our clothes. Unfortunately, when we over breathe, there is no visible cue that highlights this problem. However, as a result of over breathing, we may develop respiratory disorders, anxiety, and added stress. This chapter explores the fact that breathing more is not always a good thing. There may be moments when we need to, like when we travel to high-altitude cities or when we climb mountains, but for the most part, if our environment stays constant, we don't need to breathe consistently with no pauses after the exhale.

I call this Intermittent Breath Fasting (IBF). Right after the exhale, instead of immediately following with the next inhale, you can gently pause your breathing for a period that is reasonably comfortable and then continue with the inhale. You're not trying to break the world record here. Starting with a few counts between the last exhale and the next inhale is more than enough. As much as possible, if you can create a rhythm while trying to breathe this way during your exercises, it will help the body remember to breathe this way even when you're not paying attention to your breath. Over time, you will notice that your breathing pattern incorporates pauses effortlessly.

The more you practice breathing with intentional pauses, the more you'll become aware of the moments when you unconsciously hold your breath for long periods of time. This is not advisable but, unfortunately, it's becoming more common as we lead exceedingly busy and stressful lives. Some of us are probably aware of email or screen apnea: We stop breathing when we check our emails or watch television. Such unconscious long breath holds, or shallow breathing, is not healthy since it invigorates the sympathetic nervous system and puts us into fight-or-flight mode. Natural healing within the body takes place when we are in the parasympathetic nervous system—rest-and-digest mode. IBF allows for a rhythmic breathing pattern that puts the body into a state of relaxation since the breath hold is an extension of the exhalation.

Exercise

When you start doing this exercise, make the breathing duration between inhale (I), exhale (E), and pause (P) repetitive. The pattern would look like this:

I (4 seconds) → E (2 seconds) → P (2 seconds) →
I (4 seconds) → . . .

or

I (4 counts) → E (4 counts) → P (4 counts) →
I (4 counts) → . . .

You might struggle with either pattern and feel more comfortable with a different one. You may experiment a little until you find what works for you. During this week, I would like you to incorporate a comfortable or natural pause after every exhale. The pause becomes an extension of the exhale. Once 4 seconds are easy, you can increase the length of the pause to 5 or 6 seconds. Focus on not forcing the body but on what comes naturally to you.

Remember there's no right or wrong in terms of how long the pause is in between the inhale-exhale breath cycles. What is important is to be comfortable and to make the repetitions as rhythmic as possible. Do this exercise as often as you can because it might take a while for the brain to get used to IBF.

Over time, you'll notice that the combination of exhale and pause exceeds the counts for the inhale. When this starts happening, you may notice as well that your body is able to go deeper into relaxation. If you apply this rhythm and experience the accompanying relaxation when you're doing your cold showers, you might find you are able to lengthen the time that you're exposed to cold water.

I would encourage you to honor what your body can do at this time. If you can get at least two counts more on your exhale than you can on your inhale, that's a great start. Over time, you can naturally pause after the exhale for whatever interval seems reasonable. The key is to stay comfortable while doing these exercises. Only increase the exhale or pause counts once you feel you have mastered the previous count.

You may also progress toward incorporating pauses even when you're walking, by intentionally taking steps without inhaling or exhaling. I play around with this every time I go for a walk alone. While to everyone else I seem to be just walking, I'm actually counting my steps and playing with the combination of inhales, exhales, and pauses.

You may also incorporate this while you are praying the Hail Mary* or the Rosary. One option is to silently say "Hail Mary, full of grace, the Lord is with thee" on the inhale, "blessed are you among women" on the exhale, and "blessed is the fruit of thy womb, Jesus" on the pause after the exhale. Depending on where you are on your journey, you might be able to hold your pause for more or less time; the key is not to force it. If you notice yourself rap-

*"Hail Mary," Prayers Every Catholic Should Know, Loyola Press, accessed September 29, 2025, www.loyolapress.com/catholic-resources/prayer/traditional-catholic-prayers/prayers-every-catholic-should-know/hail-mary-prayer.

idly praying to get the words said in a single breath, you can look at breaking the line so that you can finish it in two breaths instead of one. It is imperative that you do your breathing exercises comfortably to stay in the parasympathetic nervous system that allows for the body to rest and heal.

You can also invoke the name of Jesus using this exercise. After doing an inhale and an exhale, hold a pause while saying the name of Jesus silently. As you get more comfortable with this exercise, you can invoke His name multiple times during the pause. There is power in the name of Jesus, and this would be a great way to experience the power of invoking His name. You can also practice this exercise with the Chaplet of Divine Mercy, the Angelus, the Jesus Prayer, and even the Lord's Prayer (Our Father).

If you start to enjoy being in silence and want to lengthen this time beyond what you are able to do through the exercises I've shared so far, you may influence the ratio of oxygen to carbon dioxide in your body to allow you to hold your breath a lot longer. The Wim Hof Method is one of the ways you can learn how to do this. You can access this method on the website wimhofmethod.com.

Reflection Questions

1. Did you notice the times when you were experiencing a kind of apnea: moments when you were un-

consciously holding your breath in your day-to-day activities? Were you able to break those patterns and return to breathing consciously?

2. Did you notice the body relaxing more deeply as your pauses lengthened? Did you use this exercise to help you go to sleep?
3. Did you incorporate these techniques into your prayers? What prayers did you choose? Did you use others not included here?
4. Did this technique help you stay in the cold with less resistance? Did it allow you to surrender more easily?

If you can comfortably do a cycle of I (4 counts) → E (4 counts) → P (4 counts) and catch yourself breathing this way even during your daily activities, you are ready to move to the next chapter.

8

Resting in the Lord

Experiencing Inner Stillness and Silence

Be still, and know that I am God!

—PSALM 46:10

Come to me, all you that are weary and are carrying heavy burdens, and I will give you rest.

—MATTHEW 11:28

Now that we've talked about pausing consciously between breaths, let's talk about resting there. A lot of us struggle with stress and anxiety in our daily lives, and breath is a great solution to combat it. However, "dealing with anxiety" and "resting in the Lord" are not the same. The former leads us to do the best we can while not getting enough time to heal and recover because our bodies remain in stress; the latter energizes us to deal with our interior or exterior situations with faith, knowing that God will do the heavy lifting. The latter also requires us to have good discernment in knowing what God is calling on us to do. For most of us, the scale tends to be weighted toward living a life of getting by instead of thriving and growing stronger with every passing day.

Waking up every day knowing that I am a better version of myself demands a lot of healing and recovery. It requires me to actively acknowledge that my body and mind need God's healing grace. Loving others entails a lot of effort on my part as well, and when my love is not reciprocated, I need to receive healing for that too. One way to do this is to draw inspiration to love directly from the Lord, who is abiding within me. I can do this by resting in the Lord, by being with the Lord in silence.

To know what stillness is, it's important to know what it is not. Most of us know what the lack of stillness feels like. We may think of stillness as a state that is filled with nothingness, but it can also be seen as an active state. We can be consciously still, constantly checking to make sure that the background noise in our minds is shut off, and being present to everything that is going on around us. This is great and has a lot of benefits, but resting in stillness is different. Imagine a baby lying asleep in their mother's arms or a little child sitting in silence with their head resting on their parent's chest. *Resting* means allowing ourselves to relax, recover, and refresh. The goal of this lesson is for you to experience resting in stillness, which can, for most, be harder than being actively still.

If you've been diligently following the exercises so far, there may have been times when you felt like you had zoned out or had lost count of the breaths you were taking, even though you were still doing the exercise. Runners sometimes call this a *runner's high,* and high performers tend to call this the *flow state*. If you experienced such moments, you received a glimpse of what it feels like to rest in stillness. Attaining this state requires practice and consistency. A lot of how we get to these states results from showing up every single day and, at times, moment by moment. With all the exercises you've done so far, you might notice an added sensitivity to or awareness of your new breathing pattern or generally to your internal state. You may have become more present to how the external environment affects your internal state.

In addition, the more aware we become of our breath through the exercises we have done so far, the more we are in the present moment. God can be encountered only in the present. We can also notice how movements and changes in the pace and the depth of our breathing depend on the emotions we're experiencing. If we look at the *Holy Spirit* as the parent and the *mind* and the *body* as two children, it's impossible to hear what the *Holy Spirit* has to say if the *mind* and the *body* are screaming at each other or are out of alignment. The more the two *children* listen and respond to each other, the more audible the *Holy Spirit* is, and the more we can start listening to His voice.

This is one of the goals of resting in stillness in the

presence of God: to be able to hear His voice through the stirrings of the Holy Spirit and to be able to distinguish between our own voices, the voice of God, and what is not of God. The more silence and stillness we can achieve, the greater our ability to discern. The more self-knowledge we possess, the faster we can reach the point of distinguishing between our own voices and the voice of God. The more we encounter the voice of God, the faster we can identify the voice of the evil spirit, for it does not have similar characteristics. Numerous books have been written on the discernment of spirits,* and we won't be going into the details of this topic here. However, for the novice in breath work, even beginning to learn how to be silent and still can lead to understanding one's inner stirrings, which then leads to being able to discern between the various voices that can enter our lives.

Exercise

The easiest way to know God's voice is by practicing with Scripture. Go back to the exercises that you were doing in chapter 5 or sit with your favorite verses from Scripture. After you silently say the lines on the inhale and on the exhale, in the pause after the exhale, really sit with what

*For example: Timothy M. Gallagher, *The Discernment of Spirits: An Ignatian Guide for Everyday Living* (Crossroad, 2005).

you just said. Let the experience of what you said sink into your body and, over time, allow it to sink into your heart. You'll be able to feel a difference between saying the Scripture verse silently, where it is still in the mind, and then allowing it to *sink in* to the heart.

Once you practice this as often as you can, start moving toward feeling the inhale and the exhale, allowing the experience to continue sinking in throughout the silence between the breaths as well.

If the idea of sinking in is hard to grasp, try this: Without saying any lines in your mind, feel yourself physically sink into the chair you're sitting on. You might notice a sense of weightlessness in your upper body as you sink into the chair. If you're lying on a bed, let your body sink into the bed. You will feel as though the bed is supporting the weight of your body. Even though this is what is happening, the idea of feeling yourself sink into it allows you to relax fully and for your mind to rest more. Similarly, when you say the lines, feel the words sink in to your heart to allow the mind to rest while the experience is sinking in to you.

Work on doing these exercises as often as possible. The more you allow the phrases to sink in, the more you will be able to rest in the silence between the phrases. In this chapter, you are transitioning from focusing on what happens during the active phases of breath to what happens in between breaths, during the pause phase.

At this stage, allowing the words to sink in to your body

or your heart should be done only when you are in a stationary position. You might notice that being in a quiet environment can also help the words of Jesus sink in further. Over time, neither being stationary nor in a quiet environment will be necessary.

Once you can practice this with shorter lines or verses, you can move toward doing this with other prayers, like the Hail Mary, the Jesus Prayer,* the Chaplet of Divine Mercy, and even the Lord's Prayer. Allowing these words to sink in to your heart as you are praying them is key to experiencing stillness and rest during prayer.

Of course, using this technique, you'll notice that it might take you longer to say prayers, especially the Rosary, so if you're short on time, you can choose one of the decades and allow each Hail Mary to sink in. The next time you say the Rosary,** move to another decade to meditate on so that your prayers aren't taking too much time. After a while, if you're doing these exercises regularly, you'll notice that you need less time for the prayer to sink in to your heart and you can have the experience at your regular pace for all the decades.

You may even notice a change in how you experience Holy Mass. You'll begin to grasp the sentences more deeply

*The Jesus Prayer is a simple, short prayer that can be repeated: "Lord Jesus Christ, Son of God, have mercy on me, a sinner."

**The rosary consists of five decades, with each decade containing ten Hail Marys.

and allow the experience of the saints and angels singing "*Sanctus, Sanctus, Sanctus*" ("Holy, Holy, Holy") to really sink in. Or when the consecration of the bread and wine into the body and blood of Christ happens (transubstantiation), or when you say the words "Lord, I am not worthy that You should enter under my roof, but only say the words and my soul shall be healed." These words of the Holy Mass are powerful. Allowing them to sink in to your heart and your body will amplify the effect of what you are witnessing and, eventually, experiencing.

Another way to allow for the experience to resonate is to reflect on the effects of your words, whether spoken silently or aloud. When you say "I love you" to someone, the experience within you is different depending on who you are saying these words to—for example, when you're saying them to someone you are attracted to versus saying them to your parent or a sibling. Take the time to notice such differences. Notice how you feel when you say "I love you" to Jesus. How do those words sit in your body?

You can do this with Scripture verses too. After saying a Scripture verse of your choice, ask yourself if you really believe what you said. Or is there any skepticism tied to it? It's important at this stage to feel what you're experiencing honestly, without feeling the need to change it. Some of what comes up for you at this stage might be very surprising to you, and it's okay to be surprised by your own feelings. Be patient with yourself during these moments.

Reflection Questions

1. Were you able to find a quiet environment to practice these exercises? Did the solitary silence help?
2. How was the experience of allowing the words to sink in? Were you surprised at what came up for you?
3. Did this exercise change your experience of prayer? Did you find yourself relishing the experience instead of rushing through it?
4. Did you notice yourself sinking in to your experience of the Holy Mass?

This week's exercises were challenging, so give yourself time to sit with smaller phrases before you transition to longer prayers. After about a week of practicing these exercises, you can move on to the next chapter.

9

Pain, Pain, Go Away!

Allowing for God's Healing to Enter Our Minds and Bodies

Be angry but do not sin; do not let the sun go down on your anger, and do not make room for the devil.

—EPHESIANS 4:26–27

He heals the brokenhearted,
and binds up their wounds.

—PSALM 147:3

One of the areas that most people are interested in, in the realm of breath training, is pain management. The most effective way of dealing with pain is to accept it for what it is and recognize that the body and the mind need healing. Most of us, however, want the pain to exit the body as quickly as possible and look at it as an impediment. Instead, pain can be an avenue that our bodies and minds use to convey that they need care and attention.

Pain has many layers to it, and almost all of them create a lot of discomfort. Pain can be physical, emotional, and spiritual. Scientific studies have also shown that emotional and spiritual pain can sometimes manifest themselves as physical pain in a phenomenon called *somatization,* making it exceedingly difficult to diagnose the origin. Since I love sports, pain management and recovery are crucial in enabling me to get back out and play again the next day. Pushing ourselves to do more without recovering sufficiently can lead to injury, as can the occasional misstep that causes a sprained ankle. Inflammation, instead of being just the second line of defense of the body's immune system, is now becoming a prominent problem because of our stressful lifestyles. Our bodies are triggered more often than they need to be, leading to numerous other ailments.

Breathing intentionally is the best self-care technique we can employ at any point in time. When we experience pain, our bodies go into fight-or-flight mode, which triggers us to breathe shallowly and rapidly. Healing does not occur when we are in a sympathetic (fight-or-flight) state since the body is focused on fleeing the situation we are in. *Healing occurs when we are in a parasympathetic (rest-and-digest) state.* We have already talked about the relationship between the inhale and the exhale, as well as how we can initiate rest-and-digest through breath alone, in chapter 5.

The next time you experience any sort of discomfort, be aware of the way you are breathing. If the situation allows for it, return to the exercises you practiced in chapter 5. Extending the exhale results in a relaxed state.

Now let's move to the area of emotions. When I was younger, I struggled with sharing my feelings—anyone who knows me now would not believe that I ever had a phase like this in my life! It was because I felt that sharing my feelings never really did much for me. I felt it was a waste of time. Instead of taking the time to experience fully what I was feeling, I found myself trying to change the situation so that I did not have to deal with the discomfort.

As I have grown older and made mistakes, I've realized that running away or brushing my emotions under the rug is not the best way to go about things. I have learned to accept the discomfort and find beauty in that as well, without feeling the need to change anything. This meant finding beauty in my tears and my sorrow. I gave myself permission to experience sorrow when I was not heard, recognized, or loved. Too many of us have not been loved the way we want to be loved, and our relationship with God has paid the price for it.*

Some of us have unfortunately experienced bullying,

*For more information on how our relationship with God is influenced by the love, or lack thereof, from other people, see Paul C. Vitz, *Faith of the Fatherless: The Psychology of Atheism* (Ignatius Press, 2013).

had parents who divorced, gone through our own divorce, or suffered the loss of a sibling or a child. Some of us have been betrayed, molested, or cheated on. All these incidents have long-lasting effects. Painful experiences do not even have to be this dire: Growing up in a family where you were not the favorite child can be just as traumatic as growing up without parents. All of us see our surroundings through the lens of what we have experienced in our own lives. It's not unusual to experience the pain of not feeling loved or understood by the people around us. Some of us go through our lives receiving no help at all and face the pain alone. Dealing with such pain without the help of a therapist, loving friend, or family member can be extremely hard. However, taking the time to sit with our mental and emotional pain is very important.

So, why is this vital to address? A healthy mind and a healthy body are key to feeling that we are made in the image and likeness of God. If we like only certain parts of ourselves and not all of ourselves—including our bruises and wounds—it is like saying that we do not accept all of Jesus but only certain parts of Him. It is through His wounds that we know that He is Jesus. It is through His thirst that we receive a glimpse of the pain of feeling unloved. If we can accept His thirst and His wounds, can we not accept our own?

If we can find beauty in nature when the sun sets as well as when it rises, then we can also strive to seek beauty within ourselves when we go through life's ups and downs and experience joy and sorrow in their fullness by being present with and accepting both.

Even Jesus wept. And He was perfect.

Exercise

In this lesson, we are addressing both physical and emotional pain. If the pain is in a particular area in the body, we can bring our attention to the area that's hurting and breathe specifically and intentionally, taking in large and more pronounced inhales with relaxed exhales while keeping our minds focused on that part of our body. We can even implement visualization here by imagining that the air is going directly into that part, as if there were a door and the breath is going in and out of that area through that door.

If you enjoy visualization, on your inhales, imagine sending healing waters into the area that is hurting, and on your exhales, imagine the pain leaving the body. The advantage of doing this is that it allows for more oxygen to be carried to that specific area. Tissues need oxygen to function, and they need even more oxygen to heal. Focusing your breath on a particular area while intentionally breathing can allow for this to happen. This is why athletes who have been injured sometimes sit in hyperbaric chambers, where they breathe pure oxygen in a pressurized environment that allows the blood to carry a higher amount of oxygen to the area that needs healing. It accelerates recovery. Applying cold water to the areas of your body that are in pain can help reduce inflammation and boost circulation throughout the body.

If you're suffering from cancer and you're at a treatment session, try visualizing the radiation as healing water. The easiest way to clear muddy water in a container is by pouring clean water continuously into it, which rinses out the dirt. Here, the dirt is analogous to disease. With every inhale, imagine the body welcoming healing, and with every exhale, imagine it expunging what it doesn't need.

Now, moving on to emotional pain. The goal is to identify and label what you're feeling while using the breath as an anchor. If there's something from the past that is troubling you or a recent event has left you feeling irritated, and you find you are unable to go into it because of how much discomfort it brings, try focusing on your breath.

Slowly access the area in your body or mind that is unable to express itself or wants to run away from the discomfort. If the feeling is overwhelming, focus a little more on making the exhales longer. In this case, it's fine to exhale through the mouth if the pain is very intense. Once you feel that you're ready to explore the emotion, return to your mind or body and be present to what you're feeling without judging yourself. You may feel tightness in certain body parts or feel suffocation while doing these exercises, depending on how the body has stored the emotion. Regardless of what the feeling is, direct your breath into that area and allow yourself to be present in it while keeping most of your focus on the breath. When you feel ready to access the area causing you discomfort, you can delve deeper into what you're feeling without needing to move away from the discomfort.

Over time, you might notice that a few basic areas need attention. For example, you might be angry with a friend for not showing up for lunch. You might feel that it's because this friend has not respected your time or doesn't appreciate you as much as you appreciate them. But the deeper you go into your body and your mind, you might realize that the current situation is magnified because of the times that your father didn't show up on time to pick you up from school. The anger you were unable to express back then is what is coming out toward your friend now. This is a remarkably simple example, but the more you take the time to sit with your emotions, the more you'll begin to recognize unprocessed emotions that you were unable to sit with in the past. Gradually, you'll be able to understand yourself more and experience a degree of self-knowledge that is important to enhancing your relationship with God. After all, you can experience union with God only when you're able to allow God into every aspect of your life. The emotional, physical, and mental blocks that are present within you prevent that from happening as freely or fully as it could.

At the beginning, choose simple events: being late for a meeting, experiencing bad traffic, listening to your spouse or children talk about events that are outside your comfort zone. Be in the discomfort and try to focus on the way you're breathing through the experience. Over time, you can expand the observation to experience what's going on in your body and your mind in the present moment versus trying to process it later. This would be an advanced way to apply these exercises. Your experiences with hormetic stressors will allow you to bear the discomfort better than you have in the past. Being present to emotional discomfort at the moment might be possible only after a few days of being present to your breath, slowing it down from time to time to get through the experience and then returning to it later to process what you experienced. At some point in your breath-work journey, you will be able to refrain from shutting down or running from highly uncomfortable situations. You will have the tenacity to be present to the person who requires your attention.

As with everything, this week's exercises require practice. Look at every misfortune or irritating experience from this week onward as a blessing that you can use as practice with processing negative stressors.

In summary, the initial step is observation or awareness of the discomfort associated with the stressor. Start by doing this after the event is over, and with time, you'll be able to do this while you're still experiencing the event. The next step would be to go back and forth between the feeling of discomfort and the breath, to be able to access areas of discomfort in a slow and controlled fashion. Most of the time, discomfort appears as a sense of tension in the body, and it can be in any place in the body. For me, it's usually in my heart. I feel physical pain in my heart when something or someone hurts me. When you can locate the core of the bad experience, slow down and just stay there while allowing for God's healing to enter the area. This can be done by focusing on breathing into the specific area where you are feeling tightness—for example, the upper chest, shoulders, or the ribs. In my case, I would imagine that I am breathing directly in and out of my heart in a slow fashion till I feel my heart relax. This entire process might take multiple hours, days, weeks, or months, depending on how quickly you can become aware of the discomfort you're carrying while allowing your breath to modulate your experience and recognizing that you're not in danger as you experience the discomfort.

When you first engage in such exercises, make sure that you are either in a safe place or around people you trust. Do not do these exercises around those who are a threat to your safety, whether psychologically, physically, or emotionally.

With time, this process will become second nature to you. You'll be able to do these exercises at any time and regardless of who is around you. You won't feel the need to change the situation, and instead you'll not only be able to experience healing in your own grief but to also be the hands and feet of Jesus, supporting others when they're experiencing grief and need God's healing grace. When you're able to do this, you are a beacon of light to others, for you have learned how to put the oxygen mask on yourself first so you can then tend to others during highly stressful and anxious situations.

Reflection Questions

1. For those of you who have not taken the time to access pain in your body and/or mind, this was very likely an extremely hard lesson to practice. How did you motivate yourself to do the exercises?

2. Were you able to access any trauma or pain that you didn't realize you'd been carrying?

3. Did you experience any improvement regarding a physical pain or injury after a series of exercises intentionally directed toward the specific area?

4. Did you become aware of trust issues with loved ones or even with God that you have been carrying?

5. Did allowing for healing lead to forgiving the people or situations that hurt you? Or surrendering and trusting God to take charge of situations of injustice that you experienced?

Practice compassion with yourself and listen to your body when you don't want to go deeper into the pain. It's always possible to return to the situation later and spend more time with God, recognizing that the heavy lifting is done by Him, not by you. If you feel better having a friend or a loved one close by while you're doing this exercise, please do that. Your role is only to allow God to come in and heal the areas that hurt. You will not master the practices in this chapter right away or even within a week, but over time, with consistent practice, they will get easier. These exercises will also help you discern if you may need additional help in the form of counseling and therapy. Reaching out for help may be the obvious next step. At this time, it may not be possible to seek help; in such cases, this skill can help you process pain and trauma in the interim. Of course, it's absolutely imperative that you always listen to your body and your mind at all times without feeling the need to push through. Please move to the next chapter only when you feel comfortable doing so.

10

Sacred Heart of Jesus

Accessing the Heart Physically and Spiritually

A new heart I will give you, and a new spirit I will put within you; and I will remove from your body the heart of stone and give you a heart of flesh.
—EZEKIEL 36:26

Out of the believer's heart shall flow rivers of living water.
—JOHN 7:38

In Acts 15:9, the heart is spoken of as being purified by faith. This is one of the most important lessons we receive from Jesus. Healing occurs through our faith. So, even though we may be doing the exercises diligently and correctly, our openness to hearing the voice of God and the extent to which we experience healing is determined by our faith in God's healing power. Healing also depends on how His grace wants to work in us, which usually happens organically, supporting our own interior processes and possibilities. We need to be aware that we cannot force this; it takes place in God's time. However, we are to prepare our hearts for receiving God's grace, just like a gardener prepares the soil by ensuring it is fertile, removing weeds, and watering it regularly before planting seeds to ensure healthy growth. Similarly, we can prepare to receive healing by experiencing the heart on a physical level before we are able to connect to it on a spiritual level, because *heart* can signify both the physical organ and the spiritual center of the person. The easiest way to feel your physical heart is by putting your hand on your chest, where you expect the heart to be. If you cannot feel your heartbeat, move your hand around a little until you find the spot where it is unmistakable. The way you breathe influences the way your heart beats. You can experiment with this. By breathing faster and slower, you can notice changes in your heartbeat as well.

So why is this important? Because when we're upset or frazzled, we tend to breathe more shallowly and have a higher heart rate. This sort of breathing pattern automatically puts us into the sympathetic nervous system, which then directs the flow of blood into the parts of the body that are responsible for helping us get out of a situation or to fight it. Staying in difficult situations and finding solutions requires us to breathe differently—slower and deeper—to direct the flow of the blood to the prefrontal cortex, which controls rational thought. By breathing slowly and thus relaxing the heartbeat (the physical heart), we can begin to positively influence our spiritual heart and so counter very difficult situations while maintaining a balanced interior state.

For some of us, the first time we take note of our spiritual heart is when we fall in love. Or maybe when we have an encounter with something or someone that takes over every waking moment in our lives. With me, it was my journey with tennis. Tennis was my first love. I ate, slept, and breathed tennis.

I also experienced what it meant to have a broken heart when I realized I couldn't pursue a career in tennis. Knowing my life was going to change dramatically by becoming an engineer, I decided to shut off my emotions and go about getting my degree and making my mark on the world through the energy sector.

Today, many years later, I am in touch with my spiritual heart again. God was not joking when He said He would give me a new heart, "a heart of flesh." When you are hurt and shut things out, you get a stony heart. I finally have the courage to live out my vocation. This is what happens when the heart is engaged. You feel courage and take more chances.

This is not a novel idea. In fact, most of you who are reading this are probably nodding, knowing exactly how it feels when your mind and heart are aligned. Decision-making becomes easier and faster; less energy is required to get through the day. We're generally able to make the right choices when we avoid dwelling on negative thoughts that cloud our judgment and lead us astray.

So why do we prefer to ignore our spiritual hearts? The answer is usually one of four things: (1) the discomfort of experiencing vulnerability, (2) the fear of what we might find that could lead to pain and suffering, (3) the effort it takes to access it, or (4) the view that the heart, when seen as the seat of our emotions, can lead us away from God and become an obstacle. However, the heart is also the place where God has written His covenant and where He abides.

Living a life connected to the heart is not an easy path, but it is a very fruitful one. It can be a challenge to access something that, most likely, your parents, teachers, and mentors did not show you how to experience. Over the past few lessons, these topics have been introduced for you to gain an understanding of the role your breath plays in helping you access the spiritual heart through the physical heart.

When we encounter Jesus and have a glimpse of how His heart beats in us—and *for* us—we experience the depth and infinite power of what love can feel like. No language can perfectly capture love, just as there's no language to perfectly capture what breath is. We love because our hearts were designed to give and receive love, and we breathe because we were designed by the Creator to live. I find it interesting that the words *live* and *love* have only one letter that is different. When I'm focused on the way *I* breathe and allow for the stirring of the Holy Spirit within me, focusing on the two *o*'s in l*o*ving *o*thers and being present for them becomes the default state of being.

Finally, we can pursue embodying the Sacred Heart of Jesus within us. The Sacred Heart burns with love for God the Father and for us while bleeding from the crown of thorns around it. When we connect with our hearts, our capacity to be loving while we suffer grows significantly. The more we allow for healing and love to flow through our hearts, the more this growth seems infinitely exponential. This may give us a better perspective on the seemingly endless capacity for suffering that the saints and martyrs demonstrated, which may seem supernatural. Rather than feeling intimidated by the supernatural, we can seek God's boundless grace by connecting with our hearts, allowing His healing grace to flow through us. This connection might surprise us with our capacity to forgive repeatedly, as mentioned in Matthew 18:22; from the heart, as in Matthew 18:35; and to love even amid great suffering, as illustrated in Luke 23:34.

Think about Jesus in the Divine Mercy image: He walks

toward us despite the wounds that He bears, He blesses us with the hand that carries the wound of His crucifixion, and blood and water gush out of His heart as a depiction of His grace and mercy for us. We, too, can carry Jesus in our hearts and allow for His grace and mercy to flow out of our own hearts toward those who are suffering and hurting. This is the power of being a wounded healer—we understand the other's pain through the wounds that we carry ourselves. The discomfort and the pain that we have experienced through accessing our hearts can lead to freedom and allow us to be Jesus's crucified hands and feet for others.

Exercise

As with most things in life, the exercises in this chapter require practice. There's no upper limit to the number of times you can do them. The more often, the better.

Learning how our own hearts beat is an especially important first step, much like familiarizing yourself with piano keys and the sounds they produce before playing a piece.

Your heart beats automatically. However, there is a way to influence the beating or the pace of the heart, and that is through your breath. If you were walking right now, you would be breathing at a certain pace. If you were to start running, you would notice that the pace at which you breathed and your heart beats would increase.

The easiest way to access your physical heart is by feeling your heartbeat. Earlier in this chapter, I suggested you put your hand on your chest to experience your heartbeat. Once again, try to get to the exact point on your chest where you feel the hardest thumping of your heart. Sit there for a few minutes, just feeling your heart, and then pay attention to your breath while feeling your heart. Go back and forth between your breath and your heart till it gets easier to perceive them both at the same time.

After a few days of this, try to experience your heart beating while practicing Intermittent Breath Fasting (IBF). Usually, your heartbeat feels more pronounced when you're holding your breath. With all the exercises that you have done so far, it might not be difficult to hold your breath for a little longer than usual. Prolong some of the pauses between your breaths to focus your attention completely on your heart while you hold your breath.

After a little more practice, see if you can feel your heartbeat even when you don't have your hand on your heart. This is a lot more challenging and may take quite a few attempts before you start sensing your heart beating when your hand is not on your chest. Please be patient with yourself. Another way to do this exercise is to put your middle and ring fingers on the pulse point on your neck and feel your pulse, and after a while, remove your fingers and try to experience your pulse without your fingers on the neck. Go back and forth between having your fingers on the spot and removing them until you start feeling the pulse even when your fingers are not on the spot. This takes quite a bit of practice. You can do the same on your wrist as well. For some of you, it might be easier to do this exercise with the neck and the wrist, rather than the chest.

At this point, you've done enough exercises to connect physically with your heart. Now let's explore a few options to connect with your heart spiritually.

An easy one to begin with is to imagine the heart expanding with every inhale that you take and returning to its original size with every exhale. Once you are comfortable with this visualization, you can fill your heart at every inhale with peace, worthiness, love, hope, and courage. On every exhale, let go of any fear, doubt, despair, helplessness, anxiety, or depression. You may keep connecting with the heart through your breath throughout the day. You can also set a timer for five minutes so that you can immerse yourself in the experience in solitary silence.

Another exercise you may try is to imagine Jesus's heart beating in yours. I have a great devotion to the Sacred Heart of Jesus, and it's easy for me to imagine His luminous heart beating inside of me. (If you feel a deeper connection with the Immaculate Heart of Mary, you can do the same with her heart as well.) If it's easier for you to use words to affirm the experience, you may repeat the line "O Jesus, make my heart meek and humble like Yours" with every breath. You may also say, "Beat in me, O Heart of Jesus."

Another visualization I enjoy very much is imagining that Jesus is outside the door of my heart (I do have a very ornate door to my heart!), knocking. I see Him standing at the door, and I consciously allow Him into my heart. I then watch Him walk around in my heart, touching areas of my heart that need healing and restoration. I usually end this meditation by imagining us hugging each other, with our hearts merging and beating as one. Sometimes I allow for His breath to ignite a fire within my heart, like the burning bush that Moses encountered (Exodus 3).

If you've had trauma in your life, you may imagine that you're holding your heart in your hands and seeing all the cuts and bruises that are on it while it beats timidly. You then hand your heart over to Jesus and allow Him to heal your heart with His healing touch. Often, I take time to watch Him elaborately heal each wound that I received in the past day and see the cuts and bruises miraculously vanishing. When He gives the heart back to me, my heart feels lighter and younger!

If you're struggling with forgiving loved ones who have betrayed your trust or hurt you deeply, you may visualize Jesus standing next to you as you see yourself standing opposite the person or people who have hurt you. Take the time to disclose to them how hurt you are. Once you've shared your feelings, turn to Jesus and allow His radiant golden light to flow from His heart through yours, then direct the light from your heart to the person or people who have hurt you. If you're comfortable experiencing Jesus's heart beating in your own heart, then you can experience His radiant light flowing directly from your own heart to those who have hurt you. And you can see the radiant golden light flowing from their hearts as well.

As you can see, there's no shortage of visualizations and meditations you may indulge in. The main thing to remember this week is to practice patience with yourself and to always use the breath as an anchor, especially when you begin to feel frustration at not being able to achieve what you're looking for. For some, these visualizations may come very naturally. For others, you may struggle to experience your heartbeat with your hand on your chest. Regardless, do not lose hope and continue practicing. Practice will lead to breakthroughs.

Take the time to journal your experiences. Most of us don't usually imagine another's heart within us, and for some, this can be a visceral and emotional experience, especially if you connect deeply to the crown of thorns that is depicted on His Sacred Heart. The more we can imagine His heart beating in ours, the more we will be able to embrace a deeper union with the Sacred Heart of Jesus—through suffering and glory alike.

You can also use all the knowledge shared here to prepare for difficult interactions, such as having to ask for pardon, bringing up difficult topics with others, or resolving conflict. Pre-meditating such situations may help in regulating your heartbeat while you're in the situation itself. It may also help to visualize the person you are going to talk to as a child of God and remind yourself of the positive traits in the person, while simultaneously observing your breath and your physical heartbeat. All of these tools can help the conversation to take place in a more loving and patient way. Initially, the amount of front-end work will always be greater. Over time, you will notice that you will be able to do this faster and with less conscious effort; eventually it becomes a part of who you are, not something you are striving toward.

Once again, there is no destination on such journeys. The idea is to connect with our hearts, to become aware of God's abode that exists within our hearts, and to allow for His healing grace to flow into our beings. All we need to do is to be present to the internal stirrings within our hearts, slow down our breathing, and wait for Him in faith.

Reflection Questions

1. Was accessing the heart easier or harder than accessing the mind or the body?

2. Were you able to sit with any of the meditations that were described here? Or did you create any of your own?

3. Were you able to experience healing in any way?

4. Did you become aware of events or people in your life right now that are causing you great pain? Did active healing and forgiveness allow you to approach the situation differently?

5. Did your perspective on your capacity to forgive others change? What about how tolerant you can be of others' faults?

6. During these exercises, did you find that your heart desired to receive the Sacrament of Reconciliation? Did you act upon it?

Make it a point to connect with your heart several times this week, and then spend some time in quiet solitude to deeply engage with the reflections discussed here. I encourage you to come up with your own. If these visualizations aren't working well for you, even the act of having your hand on your heart and being present with your heartbeat is a good place to be. After about a week of doing this, you may progress to the next chapter.

11

The Return of the Two Sons

Experiencing Our Father's Love

The Lord is good;
his steadfast love endures forever.
—PSALM 100:5

Those who wait for the Lord shall renew their strength,
they shall mount up with wings like eagles,
they shall run and not be weary,
they shall walk and not faint.
—ISAIAH 40:31

As Christians, we know that we are to practice love toward God and toward our neighbor. Jesus talks about it clearly in Matthew 22: "You shall love the Lord your God with all your heart, and with all your soul, and with all your mind" (verse 37). Then He says, "You shall love your neighbor as yourself" (verse 39). This second commandment get harder when Jesus tells us, "Just as I have loved you, you also should love one another" (John 13:34).

How can I know what it means to love unless I have experienced what it feels like to be loved? Ideally, this happens when we are children, and parents are meant to be the image of what God's love looks like. And yet, they often fall short. Our parents do the best they can, but sometimes their best is not what we consider love. And then there is unconditional love, *agape*. How many times have we experienced *agape*?

So, going back to the commandments, how am I to fulfill the first commandment if, deep down, I have not experienced God's unconditional love?

In my humanity, the extent to which I can abandon myself to the love and care of another person is dependent on how much love and care I receive from this relationship. It depends on faith, trust, and my past experiences. It also depends on whether I can heal from painful incidents and if I'm willing to give the relationship another shot, fully acknowledging that I can get hurt just the same, if not more, in the future. Of course, I'm not referring to relationships that are abusive or threaten our existence, but rather the pain that we experience in relationships when people hurt us unknowingly or refuse to apologize when they know that we are hurt. There is also the pain that comes from wanting to intentionally hurt another because we are in pain. Hence the saying *"Hurt people* hurt people."

Is it possible to love despite the pain? Yes, it is. This is what Jesus did for us. However, it's extremely hard to do so without allowing God's healing grace into our lives. And we cannot do that unless we first have an encounter with Jesus. Most of us have had more encounters with people or things that have caused us pain than with saints or angels who have been able to reflect God's love to us.

Even though Scripture is a great way to encounter Jesus, most of us experience God through our encounters with others. We make the decision to leave or stay in the kingdom based on such encounters. This topic is so important that I decided to write a whole chapter on it. If you are reading this, then *you* are called to love. *You* are called to treat your family and friends with love. *You* are called to break the pattern of people not encountering saints. *You* are called to be Mary who brought Jesus into this world. *You* are called to be Jesus's hands and feet. *You* are called to act! Instead of waiting for the pope, priests, and religious brothers and sisters to step up, we all need to step up through our immediate relationships. If you've mastered every breathing exercise and finished this book merely as a method to manage anxiety, you've missed the point: Breathing fosters internal healing, enabling us to support others in their healing journey. It helps us connect with our own hearts, which in turn allows us to connect with the hearts of others.

Breathing helps us experience God. We cannot see our breath just as we cannot see God. Yet, no matter what is going on in our lives, we always have breath and we always have God. We need breath to live and God to love. God is as essential to us as breath. Without breath, there is no life; without God, there is no meaning to our lives.

I often hear people say that converts have the most zeal. By *converts,* I'm not referring only to people who have had a change of religion (like me) but also people who have had a divine encounter that brought them to the Holy Eucharist with renewed zeal. I believe this could be the case because many of us tend to associate ourselves with the prodigal son, the lost sheep, or the Samaritan woman. If you're unfamiliar with the parable of the prodigal son, read Luke 15:11–32. Most converts will tell you that they either received something that brought immense healing to their hearts or had an actual encounter with Jesus, which showed them that He is the way, the truth, and the life. In my case, I had both, which sealed the deal for me, and I didn't have to seek anymore. I was looking for truth and for love, and I found them both in Jesus. Through the Sacraments of Reconciliation and the Holy Eucharist, I have access to the body, blood, soul, and divinity of Christ every day. As prodigal sons and daughters, we go to God with our tails between our legs, expecting scraps, and instead receive our Father running toward us with open arms, throwing a feast in our honor!

There is another son in this story, the older son, who is just as loved by his father but does not fully understand the depth and breadth of his father's love. This son seems to have no issue sticking by his father, leading a life following the rules, acknowledging that he is protected in his father's house. He finds it difficult to love his younger brother and does not celebrate his return, as it is challenging to love those who have hurt our loved ones, ignored the rules we have faithfully followed, and yet seem to receive more love and attention than we do. This is hard to digest, and I think we can all relate to the older brother, convert or not. Yet once there is a level of faith present within us that allows us to believe that we are indeed loved, watching the joy of our loved ones is enough for us to be joyous and leads us to want to share the joy that is present.

In this parable, neither of the sons understood their father. While the younger son timidly comes back, not expecting to receive the welcome that he does from the father, the older brother is disappointed that his younger brother receives something that he never had. Neither of them fully understands the depth and breadth of their father's love. Most of us do not either. For the younger son, it would mean not hesitating even for a single second, rushing back to his father, knowing that he'll be welcomed with open arms, and then recognizing the value of being in his father's house and never wanting to leave again. For the older son, it means recognizing that his father's love for him never changes, regardless of whoever else enters the house.

This is what Jesus did for us. Jesus knew how much joy it would bring His Father if He loved His brothers and sisters with the same love that His Father has for us, and so He left the kingdom momentarily to lay down His own life so that we, too, can join Him in His Father's kingdom. He does this out of love for His Father, for He knows the joy that His Father experiences when His sons and daughters return to Him. When we love someone that much, we are willing to do anything to see joy in that person's eyes. Jesus was willing to give up His own life to see us enter the kingdom.

Jesus's and Mother Mary's love for God the Father gave them the power, the courage, and the strength to live a life that was unconventional. Their choices in life resulted in extreme pain, but no amount of pain and suffering could extinguish the love they carried in their hearts for God the Father. This is why we're able to go to them, trusting that they truly do want the best for us and want us to experience God's love. This holds true for the saints whom we venerate within our Catholic Church as well. It is clear from the way the saints express themselves and the way Jesus talks about His Father that they had indeed encountered God's love for them firsthand. Through the love of Jesus, they had access to the rivers of living water, which gushed out of their own hearts (John 7:38).

This kind of love is what we long for. This love banishes fear, moves past judgment, treats others with dignity and respect, breaks all societal barriers, and looks past people's wealth or lack thereof. This kind of love does not compare or make us feel that we are less than when we are not celebrated. It stops us from gossiping about others and allows us to forgive those who have hurt us and our loved ones. It gives us the strength to ask for forgiveness when we have wronged another. It allows us to stay up all night listening to a friend cry or risk our own health while caring for a sick friend. This love allows us to love with the Father's love.

The two commandments are dependent on each other. You cannot have one without the other.

Now read 1 John 4:18–21 considering everything you have read so far.

> There is no fear in love, but perfect love casts out fear; for fear has to do with punishment, and whoever fears has not reached perfection in love. We love [God] because he first loved us. Those who say, "I love God," and hate their brothers or sisters, are liars; for those who do not love a brother or sister whom they have seen, cannot love God whom they

> have not seen. The commandment we have from him is this: those who love God must love their brothers and sisters also.

The first time I understood the love that was present between the Father and the Son and that we were being invited to partake in this through the Holy Spirit, I cried for days, not being able to believe the gift that had been bestowed on us. This was the fatted calf, killed for me! The divine wedding banquet that I was invited to! Oh, how unworthy I felt to receive such an honor, but at the same time, I was overjoyed that I could finally rest in my Father's open arms and experience His healing, nourishing, and rejuvenating love.

I am both the younger and the older brother. As the younger brother, I have been made aware time and again of my sinful nature and how far I have walked away from my Father before I felt the need to return. As the older brother, I have been irritated with cradle Catholics for their lack of knowledge of Scripture and have expected more charity to be present in the Catholic Church. I have also been disappointed with people's lack of belief in the Eucharist. When we meet others, we meet both the older and the younger brother in the same person. Sometimes, we can go back and forth between the older and younger brother multiple times throughout the day!

So how do we consistently remind ourselves that we

are indeed called to love with the Father's love and not be content as either the older or the younger brother? Through *breath.* I look at every breath that I take in as an opportunity to connect with the intentions of my actions and my words. Am I being like one of the brothers through the words that I say and the thoughts that I have? What could I think or say to act more like my Father? How quickly can I run back without hesitation to my Father's arms to rest there, have my wounds tended to, experience healing, and remember that I am a child of God? I know I need to do this before I understand how to love as He loves.

The idea of God's arms being open for me always reminds me of the shape of my ribs. My ribs expand with every inhale that I take. At every inhale, I experience God's open arms; at every exhale, I allow myself to be hugged by Him; at every pause in my breathing, I allow myself to sink deeper into His arms and rest there. Whether I am aware of my mistakes or have done good deeds to impress Him and prove my worthiness does not matter. I am His daughter, and He loves me. The act of resting in His arms is acknowledging that fact.

If we believe that God is the one who gives us life and keeps us alive constantly, then He does so by allowing our hearts to beat, by providing us with life-sustaining air as we breathe in, and by freeing us from what is not needed in our body as we breathe out. We can experience His loving embrace in our bodies as soon as we perceive Him in this way.

Only when we experience this kind of love—God's love—can we then love unconditionally. Unconditional love does not mean you do not address people's mistakes. Instead, it means to correct others with love, to feel responsible for all our brothers and sisters, and to acknowledge that we are accountable for our family members' salvation. Jesus felt responsible for us. He expects us to feel responsible for our loved ones as well.

It is not possible to give what we have not received—and sometimes refuse to receive—because we feel we are unworthy to receive it. I pray that, through these exercises, we allow for God's healing grace and love to enter our lives through His open arms.

Exercise

These practices are all about the intentionality of the thoughts that are in our minds when we breathe. Experiencing the Father's arms around us, wrapping us in a big hug and allowing us to rest in His arms while we breathe—regardless of anything good or bad happening in our lives—is also a question of our awareness and of our consciously allowing ourselves to be received by the Father. The consistent awareness of His presence in our very breath is a powerful way to remember that we always have a way to connect with the Father.

The image of my ribs expanding as His arms wrap around me is what has helped me, but you may use any image of your liking. The more you can experience His arms around you for no reason at all, the easier it will be for you to believe in God's love as a constant in your life. Many of us have not had such relationships in our lives; we've had to earn our love, and so we need to first believe in this kind of unconditional love from God before we can work on loving others this way.

Some people have told me that they received unconditional love from their mother, not their father. Experiencing God as father is difficult for them. If you are this person, then know that God is beyond gender. Man and woman are made in the image and likeness of Him, and so God is our all in all. What is important is to know that you have someone you can run to, and God is waiting for you with open arms.

Another way to experience God's love and healing is by saying the Lord's Prayer (Matthew 6:9–13). I have broken down the "Our Father" prayer using this chapter's underlying theme of the two brothers, and I would encourage you to read the explanation along with every line, followed by closing your eyes. Connect with the heart as you have previously learned and allow yourself to sink into each phrase fully.

"Our Father"—In the past, I interpreted this line to mean that all who I encounter are my brothers and sisters. Now I make it more personal and recognize this is the moment of reconciliation between both the older and the younger brother within me. I visualize them hugging each other in joy at the banquet, praying together, and celebrating with their father. I acknowledge that this is what brings the greatest joy to my Father: seeing the younger and older brother within me reconciled.

"Who art in heaven"—This is my reminder that I do not want to leave my Father's kingdom. I recognize that I have left it numerous times (by committing sin), and it has caused both me and my Father a lot of pain and anguish. I also recognize that there have been times when I have taken the kingdom for granted, not being joyful for others entering and celebrating in their victories. There is no other place I want to be than in my Father's arms and in His kingdom.

"Hallowed be thy name"—Is such a Father not worthy of praise? One whose arms are forever open for me and whose desire is that I dwell in His kingdom? I have never experienced this kind of acceptance from anyone else. I want Him to know how in awe of Him I am! How much I yearn to praise Him to everyone I meet.

"Thy kingdom come"—Here I ask God to show me how to love like Him, with the Father's love, so that I, like Jesus, can bring the love and desire to build His kingdom to others.

"Thy will be done"—I understand that God's will, as expressed in the commandments and the voice in my conscience, is not easy to follow and may be uncomfortable at times, especially as it relates to love and forgiveness, yet my joy that comes from being close to Him and surrendering my will to His overshadows the discomfort.

"On earth, as it is in heaven"—I have faith that by living this way, I will experience heavenly joy in my earthly life.

"Give us this day our daily bread"—Here, I thank God for the fatted calf and the wedding banquet. Every time I come back to His open arms, I cannot believe how much God celebrates my homecoming! I never get used to it and look forward to it every single time I rest in His arms. I am also secure in the love that my Father has for me and that He always provides for all my needs.

"And forgive us our trespasses"—I acknowledge that I need God's forgiveness, for times when my leaving Him has caused immense pain and distress. I know God hurts knowing that I feel unworthy of receiving His love. He also hurts when I am unable to love others when I experience their weaknesses, faults, or mistakes. He helps me to remember that He is always waiting to bestow on me the absolution of my sins in the Sacrament of Reconciliation.

"As we forgive those who trespass against us"—I ask the Father for grace to forgive those who weren't there to rejoice with me when I repented of my sins and went back to Him. I ask for the grace to forgive those who have not celebrated with me the way He does or have not loved me, embraced me, and understood me the way He does. I also ask for help to forgive those who seem to be wayward and sinful, to understand that He does not stop bestowing on them His unconditional love and mercy, and to accept that He is inviting me to do the same, without judging them. I trust that God's mercy will be just and that His justice will be merciful. (If anyone specific comes to mind during this portion of the prayer, you may stay here for some time and really work on forgiving the person(s) as explained in chapter 9.)

"And lead us not into temptation"—I recognize that I will continue to face temptations to stray from the kingdom, even though I know it has never served me in the past. I am also aware that I may have the temptation of seeing myself as better than others. Here I ask the Father for the grace never to

> take His love for granted. I always want to remember that He is waiting for me with open arms regardless of how unworthy and tarnished I feel.
>
> "But deliver us from evil"—With every breath I take, I sink deeper into the embrace of my beloved Father. I feel clean. White as snow. I feel my wounds healing, and I am experiencing the nourishing and joyful experience of being one with Him again and the beating of our hearts as one.

This week, try to pray the "Our Father" at least once a day, while resting with each line intentionally. If you can do this at the same time every day, that would be ideal. The body loves to have a routine, and it is easier for the spiritual heart to be engaged and ready when an exercise is being done at the same time every day. As always, this is only an example; you might start realizing that there are no limits to the prayers you can do this with. With practice, you'll get to the point that you do this with every prayer.

Take, for example, the mysteries of the holy Rosary. There are so many ways that we can go deeper into these mysteries using our breath. The Rosary is an easy way to access our hearts to take note of where we need healing. One of my favorite ways to do this is to allow for the fruit of the decade to sink into my heart, and it inevitably will bring up a time when I felt humiliated, when I needed strength to carry my cross, or when I haven't been very charitable to my neighbor. I am immediately made aware of either the healing that is needed in that area or the shift in attitude that is needed to become more Christlike.

This might not be your experience right off the bat, but exercising patience with yourself will allow for the heart to open, and over time, the heart will feel comfortable to share more with you. You will become strong enough to become aware of areas that need healing as well as areas where gentle correction is needed. Your spiritual heart starts opening up to you when you don't feel judged as weak or identified with the younger or the older brother. In many ways, you are to emulate the love of the Father toward your own heart. Another way to look at this is to allow the doctor to stitch up your wound. This requires you to reveal the wound to them. In addition to the discomfort of revealing the wound, it is very painful when the wound is accessed, especially without anesthesia. But allowing the doctor to access it is the first step toward healing.

Similarly, God knows where we need healing, and yet it's our acknowledgment that we need healing and our showing the wound to God that starts the healing process. The act of resting in His arms, experiencing His love, is anesthesia while He tends to our wounds.

Breathing not only allows us to manage the anxiety related to revealing the wound, but it also helps reduce the pain experienced when the wound is accessed. By breathing intentionally and making your exhales longer than your inhales, you can continue to keep the body in a relaxed parasympathetic state, which allows for healing to occur.

Reflection Questions

1. Has there been a change in the way you look at God? Are you allowing Him into areas of your daily life? Or do you approach Him only when you feel you have no other way to move forward?
2. How easy or hard was it for you to open your heart during prayer and allow yourself to sink into our Father's arms? Did it require a lot of time? Did the amount of time and effort lessen over a week of practicing this?
3. What other visualization did you use to remind yourself of God's love for you?
4. Were you able to see both the younger son and the older son within you? (You may write down ways you see both within you. You may even ask your loved ones to help you with this reflection question.) How did encountering both within you help you become more present to the Father's love?

Take your time with this week's exercises. If you need to practice them for two weeks, please do so. They can be implemented as often as you like. If, after about two weeks, you still feel unsure, continue reading the book and keep practicing this week's exercises once you've finished.

12

Love for Our Father

Encountering the Eucharist with Love

Those who eat my flesh and drink my blood abide in me, and I in them.

—JOHN 6:56

You shall not change Me [Jesus] into yourself as bodily food, but into Me you shall be changed.

—SAINT AUGUSTINE, *CONFESSIONS*

Until now, the focus has mainly been on allowing God into our lives and allowing Him to abide in our hearts while we experience His healing grace in our lives. This chapter focuses on how we can show our love for God. In Luke 17:11–19, only one of the ten lepers went back to thank Jesus for the healing he received. We want to be like that one leper who returned to thank the Lord.

The word *Eucharist* comes from the Greek word "*eucharistia,*" which means "thanksgiving."* What are we giving thanks for? We are giving thanks for the sacrifice that Jesus made by giving up His life on the cross so that we could be His adopted brothers and sisters who have access to the kingdom of God. One way of showing God that we love Him is by receiving His Son's body and blood.

Imagine if your mother went to work every day, toiling to buy you a pair of shoes. Would it not give her happiness to see you wearing the shoes every time you went out? You might also want to wear the shoes to show your appreciation for what she did for you.

Consider, too, how the joy we feel when we receive a gift increases exponentially when we're aware of the effort that the giver has put into the gift. This is why we value the time and effort someone invests in creating something special for us. We hope this is why men put so much thought and so many resources into buying a ring for the woman they want to marry, for it shows the man's commitment to his future wife. And the wife joyfully wears the ring to constantly remind her of the commitment that was made between her and her husband.

In the same way, God made the ultimate sacrifice in of-

*Strong's, "Eucharist," https://biblehub.com/greek/2169.htm.

fering His only begotten Son to renew the covenant of us being His own. Jesus did this out of love for His Father and for us. Receiving this priceless gift is one way to express our gratitude and love to both Jesus and our Father.

Occasionally, we take the gifts we receive and our relationships for granted, and so it is no surprise that we may also take the Eucharist for granted. Through grace that we receive from God, we come to believe that the Eucharist is the body, blood, soul, and divinity of our Lord Jesus Christ.

If you're struggling to believe this, don't hesitate to ask God to reveal Himself to you in prayer. You may also read about the vast number of Eucharistic miracles that have occurred and consider visiting a few of these sites to see these miracles in person. Saint Carlos Acutis created a miracles list and published it on this website: Miracolieucaristici.org. For now, as you do your breathing exercises to connect with your heart, ask God to reveal Himself to you through the Eucharist in His time. Sometimes the hardest step is to give the Holy Eucharist one more try if you have never encountered Christ this way. I once heard a priest say that waiting for the Lord is like keeping the door unlocked so that at any time, the Lord could walk into your room. The act of keeping the door unlocked is the act of faith that we make through prayer, and it helps us to appreciate the gift that we receive through Holy Mass.

No one can tell you how to fall in love with Christ in the

Eucharist, for each one of us has a unique relationship with God. However, I would like to share some of my personal anecdotes on how I have encountered Christ in the Eucharist and how these experiences have deepened my faith in the gift that we receive. These experiences happened at various times during my journey in the Catholic Church.

Often, after receiving the Eucharist and returning to my pew, I say the words *Now that I have consumed You, now, You, please consume me. O Lord, consume all of me.*

I usually allow for the Eucharist to disintegrate slowly and only through my saliva so that I can feel the presence of Christ within me for a long time before I swallow all the bits and pieces that remain. During these moments, I relish the Eucharist and allow for the union between us to linger for as long as possible.

There have been times, after receiving the Eucharist, when I have spontaneously experienced Jesus and me dancing together. It was so graceful, and our steps were in absolute harmony. On other occasions, I have experienced laying my head on His chest and resting in His arms as He strokes my hair. These moments were never orchestrated or planned, and the spontaneity of their appearances always brought lasting joy to my heart.

Taking the time to relish the experience of the Eucharist is so important. Otherwise, it can end up being a checking-the-box exercise.

It still baffles me that I can consume God. Or that I can sit in the presence of God through Adoration. As Catholics, we get to see God and experience Him face-to-face. Having done intentional breathing exercises for almost a year, it was easy for me to sit in silence in front of the monstrance for forty-five to sixty minutes. I felt my thoughts vanish as soon as I sat in front of Him.

You, too, will notice that doing the exercises in this book will make it easier for you to be in Adoration and to allow yourself to be engulfed by the presence of Christ, without feeling the need to fill the hour with a book to read or a Rosary to pray. It's not that these acts are wrong; rather, we do them because we struggle to sit in silence, enjoying solely the Lord's presence. Even the simple act of invoking the name of Jesus with every breath that we take during Holy Hour can be such a powerful experience.

The way we encounter the Eucharist can also make an impact on how we encounter our loved ones. When I look at the friends who would go the extra mile for me, who are present, and who listen when I share the sorrows I carry in my heart, I pray in thanksgiving for such beautiful friends. We share a mutual love and respect for one another.

Using our breath as an anchor is one way to remind ourselves who we are sitting in front of or whom we are consuming. Sometimes, we go through Holy Mass and Adoration on autopilot, without realizing that God is aware of how distracted we are. He is always aware when we're not paying attention to Him. This would be like going on a date with your significant other and watching them scroll on their phone or look at other men and women around them when they should be appreciating your presence.

Holy Mass and Adoration are our opportunities to pay attention to God. Receiving the Holy Eucharist is a great way to acknowledge that we are joining our body, blood, and soul—our entire being—with that of Christ. In that moment, then, within your body, you can quietly experience a happy dance to celebrate the occasion! Whichever way you celebrate, remember God knows your love language. All He wants is to feel loved, and there are countless ways you can show Him your love. Start by doing one small thing for Him in love, even if it's allowing for one breath to expand your heart in love for Him; the rest will follow.

During a retreat that I was giving on breath, I shared Mother Teresa of Calcutta's famous line: "Do small things with great love." I reminded everyone that the smallest thing we could do with love was to breathe for God. If we could breathe even one breath of ours for God, what smaller thing could there be? From there, if we could then breathe every breath of ours for God, wouldn't that be another way of praying unceasingly?

Connecting with our breath from time to time throughout Holy Mass or using the moments when we sing hymns can make a huge difference in really waking up to what is happening around us. During Benediction, I especially enjoy the moment when Jesus Himself blesses us. I take the time to make the sign of the cross slowly across my body, allowing my hand to touch my forehead, my heart, my left shoulder, and then my right shoulder in slow motion. I usually inhale when I touch my forehead, exhale when I touch my heart, inhale when I touch my left shoulder, and exhale when I touch my right shoulder. When I touch my forehead, I am aware of the love that God the Father has for me, reflecting on His arms that are always wide and open for me to run into. When I touch my heart, I acknowledge the presence of Jesus abiding in my heart. When I move my hand from my left to my right shoulder, I thank the Holy Spirit for being the reason that I can partake in this beautiful relationship between the Father and the Son and for allowing that love to spread from my heart to my brothers and sisters who are present in my life.

The sign of the cross also reminds me of the alignment I need between my mind (when I put my hand to my forehead) and my heart (when I touch my heart) to become present to the stirrings of the Spirit within me (when I move my hand from one shoulder to the other).

Think of the number of opportunities we have to show God that we love Him. Every breath matters and every breath is a new opportunity to connect with our hearts and with God. The more you use your breath to access your heart, the more you can consciously experience the power of the Holy Spirit moving within you. Persevere in your practice, and you will be pleasantly surprised at the different ways that God walks through the unlocked door of your heart.

Exercise

In this final week, revisit each exercise from the past eleven weeks and focus on your breathing while performing them. Pay attention to the exercises you find challenging and observe the discomfort they cause. This will increase your awareness of activities you tend to avoid due to their complexity or difficulty. Once you're comfortable with these exercises, proceed to sit in silence for at least ten to fifteen minutes in the beginning, then thirty to forty minutes, and eventually forty-five to sixty minutes. Sitting in Adoration would be a great way to practice this. Once again, start slowly and become comfortable sitting in a place without feeling the need to write, talk to anyone, or read during that time. Over time, sitting in periods of silence will become easier. When the need to talk to someone, to journal, or to look at your phone goes away, slowly build on that time. With more practice, you will notice that you can engage in such periods of silence even when busy. After your period of stillness, you can journal about your experience. Have faith that the experiences during your period of silence that you forget afterward were meant to be present only during that time and have served their purpose.

Also, when receiving Holy Communion, relish the experience of being in union with God. I've given you a few examples from my own experience, but if you can rest in stillness and connect with your heart, the possibilities are limitless. If you don't believe in the true presence of Christ in the Eucharist, don't hesitate to ask for this gift in prayer. Jesus did say, "Whatever you ask for in prayer, believe that you have received it, and it will be yours" (Mark 11:24). Asking to find the true presence of Christ in the Eucharist, in my humble opinion, is a worthwhile request.

You can also practice keeping your eyes on Christ when you're in Adoration. Simply believing that Christ is indeed sitting in front of you, as you would sit in front of your loved one at a restaurant, allows you to keep your eyes on Him, even if you have a million things going on in your mind. Allow for the breath to help you settle and feel free to occasionally close your eyes, rest in the Lord, and open them back up again to focus your eyes on Him. Over time, you will feel "the eyes of your heart" open, as Saint Paul states in Ephesians 1:18, and you will no longer need your physical eyes to see Him.

Allow your perseverance in enhancing your relationship with God to flow into the relationships you have with your family and friends. Give them your undivided attention. Your relationship with your family will affect the relationship you have with God and vice versa. Pay attention to how you breathe when you are with your family, as discussed in some of the previous chapters.

Finally, don't hesitate to run to the arms of our Father through the Sacrament of Reconciliation. While you're being absolved of your sins, allow the healing grace of Jesus to wash you clean and relish this experience as you step out of the confessional. I have walked out many times with a lighter chest and a vibrant heart, enveloped in my Father's arms with joy and love, which leads to added intimacy when I receive the Holy Eucharist.

Reflection Questions

1. How does it feel to be at the end of this book? Do you feel a sense of achievement?
2. What have your major takeaways been on this journey?

Don't hesitate to pick this book up at any point to review specific exercises. Return to it at least once a year at a set time, as it can help you choose a new focus the next time around. The journey with breath is a marathon, not a sprint, so pace yourself. The summary beginning on page 119 is designed to help you quickly remember the breath-work exercises practiced. Thank you for allowing me to share this journey with you!

Conclusion

Here we are! You made it! Well done!

Realize that the journey doesn't end here. Don't let that overwhelm or intimidate you. Thankfully, you can now use your breath to experience your emotions and be present with them fully!

This would be a great time to go back to the original questionnaire and make a note of how far you've come since you answered the questions for the first time. Have you noticed any other changes besides the ones you have recorded so far in the questionnaire?

In Scripture, we are called to "pray without ceasing" (1 Thessalonians 5:17). Jesus also said, "Blessed rather are those who hear the word of God and obey it!" (Luke 11:28). There are many ways to walk such a path. The way I walked mine was to understand my breath better, first from learning how to do it, then making it an integral part of my life, then being able to sit in silence, hear the voice of God, and eventually strive toward praying without ceasing.

Self-awareness has been key in my journey to experiencing God abiding within me and, thereafter, being able to *decrease* so that God can *increase*. To be like John the Baptist, to go before the Lord to prepare His way, you have to understand what part of yourself you're attempting to decrease in order to allow for Him to increase in you. It's impossible to decrease something you're not aware of or don't understand. Breathing intentionally will build your awareness of your thoughts and deeds, which may open up an avenue of bringing subtle changes in your day-to-day activities when you feel called to do so.

Taking the time to understand how you think and feel is crucial to allowing God more fully into all of your life, not only parts of it.

Ultimately, if your journey with breath through this book has increased your awareness of both self and of other, and God has taken this opportunity to reveal Himself to you either through the Eucharist or in other ways, this book has fulfilled its purpose. Do not underestimate the healing power of being connected to the Holy Spirit through your breath. I pray that you have the self-discipline to continue the journey of breath for the sake of the journey and not the outcome.

You never know when God will show up during your daily life. Always being connected to your breath gives you the opportunity to be vigilant and ready to acknowledge His presence when His merciful providence decides to allow you to experience Him more clearly. In a way, connecting to your breath is a way to connect with the Holy Spirit intentionally, and this could be another way to experience the presence of God at all times.

One of my favorite exercises is to ask my close friends which areas in my life they would like to see me change. The more self-aware I am, the less surprised I am at their feedback. Ultimately, we have free will to choose, and the more we understand ourselves, the easier it gets to invite God into our lives and surrender to Him in childlike abandon.

> Truly I tell you, unless you change and become like children, you will never enter the kingdom of heaven. (Matthew 18:3)

May you breathe consciously, strive to pray unceasingly, and allow yourself to love and be loved wholeheartedly.

To God be all the praise and all the glory.

Summary

Breath in General

Genesis 2:7—God breathed into us! Breath brought us to life!

- God and breath are always present within us, whether we are aware of them or not; we can find them wherever we go.
- Breath brings us back to the present moment; God is experienced in the present.
- Without breath, we die; without God, we live a purposeless (dead) life.
- Breath is the easiest way to access our physical hearts; God abides in our spiritual hearts.

Connection Between Body, Mind, and the Holy Spirit

To hear the voice of the Holy Spirit, it helps to have the mind and the body aligned. Body and mind are constantly battling with each other, whether it is through our disordered passions or lack of self-discipline, and as a result, it's hard to hear the silent voice of the Holy Spirit. Breath helps with bringing about an alignment between mind and body. We do this by learning how to understand these aspects of ourselves in both the physical and the spiritual realms.

Conscious Self-Examination

How self-aware are you?

- Physical: Do I experience pain in my body? Do I have diseases that I am carrying or taking medication for?
- Mental: Am I struggling with depression, loneliness, anxiety, or suicidal thoughts?
- Emotional: Do I experience the full spectrum of my feelings? Do I feel ashamed or find it hard to share my thoughts and feelings with others? Is it hard for me to deal with my emotions without hurting myself or others?
- Spiritual: Do I believe in God? Do I trust Him? Is God an overwhelming authority or a loving parent? Do I experience His presence? Have I experienced the stirring of the Holy Spirit in my life? Am I able to hear the voice of God in my heart? Where is God in my life—is He welcome in all aspects of my life?

Or do I approach God only when I am at a loss on how to move forward?

Phases Usually Experienced Doing the Exercises

Doing the exercises in this book, you may experience some of the following:

- Humility through self-knowledge—acknowledging that you may not have been doing a lot of things correctly.
- Awareness of when you are and are not doing the exercises. These are equally important.
- Greater self-discipline.
- Changes in your emotional, physical, and spiritual realms, leading to an added zeal to continue doing the exercises.
- No significant change, but you continue to do the exercises because you are convinced that breathing can have a positive impact on your health.
- A desire to experience unconditional love and to be more intentional about loving God.
- Greater presence in setting different intentions with added awareness of areas in your life you would like to make subtle changes in.

If you've had no previous breathing experience, these exercises should be done over a ten-to-twelve-week span, which corresponds to around seventy to eighty-four days. Recent studies show that we need about sixty-seven days for a new behavior to become habitual,* and therefore, it's imperative that you do the exercises consistently so that they become a way of life. To train in sport, you shoot the same hoop or hit the same shot over and over until it becomes a part of your muscle memory so that, in a match or tournament setting, you can do the same without having to think about it. It's the same with breathing.

Pray for the guidance of the Holy Spirit before starting the exercises in the book.

Always remember:

- Consistency is more important than perfection.
- Slowing down is better than speeding up.
- Do not skip ahead in the exercises since they are meant to build on each other.
- It is important to have a daily routine to experience the stages within you.

*Jocelyn Solis-Moreira, "How Long Does It Really Take to Form a Habit?," *Scientific American,* www.scientificamerican.com/article/how-long-does-it-really-take-to-form-a-habit.

Chapter-by-Chapter Exercises

CHAPTER 1

The Fall

Setting Yourself Up for Success

- Remember that the falls are just as important as the times when you rise.
- Test your respiratory rate.
- Notice movements in your body when you inhale and exhale.
- Become aware of your breath.
- Set an alarm to remind you to practice your breath work.
- Associate your exercise with an activity that is already a part of your routine.
- Don't focus yet on the *how*.

CHAPTER 2

Wide Gate Versus Narrow Gate

Breathing Through the Mouth and Through the Nose

- Learn all about the advantages of nose breathing:
  - produces a stronger diaphragm
  - may alleviate orthodontic issues
  - reduces allergies
  - enhances the respiratory system (and produces a greater VO_2 max)
- Practice placing the tongue on your palate by saying the letter *N*.
- Learn to curtail excessive yawning.
- Use exercises to unblock your nose naturally.

CHAPTER 3

Silent Night, Holy Night

Silent and Relaxed Breathing

- Make no sound while breathing by slowing down your inhale and exhale.
- Notice the correlation between your breath rate and your heart rate.
- Learn why a resting heart rate in a healthy person often denotes a healthier heart.

CHAPTER 4

Put Out into the Deep

Breathing Deep and with Intention

- Notice the depth of your breath.
- Learn how to breathe three-dimensionally.
- Know the importance of mobility in your breathing.
- Start breathing intentionally while walking.
- Retest your respiratory rate.

CHAPTER 5

Two Sides of the Same Coin

Relationship Between the Inhale and the Exhale

- Recognize that the nervous system has two distinct states:
    - fight-or-flight (sympathetic)
    - rest-and-digest (parasympathetic)
- Relax by trying a shorter inhale and longer exhale.
- Invigorate by trying a longer inhale and shorter exhale.
- Create a calm state with an equal inhale and exhale.
- Try box breathing and 4-7-8 breathing.
- Use Scripture verses to modulate breathing and add a spiritual dimension.

CHAPTER 6

Finding Comfort in Discomfort

The Impact of Positive Stressors on Resilience

- Recalibrate the nervous system.
- Utilize hormesis: "What doesn't kill us makes us stronger!"
- Try cold exposure or walking barefoot outdoors.
- Do small things that challenge you physically and mentally.

CHAPTER 7

Fasting

Intermittent Breath Fasting (IBF)

- Learn that less can be more.
- Know the difference between breath holding and apnea.
- Incorporate prayers:
  - Hail Mary
  - the holy name of Jesus
  - Jesus Prayer
  - the Lord's Prayer
  - Angelus

CHAPTER 8

Resting in the Lord

Experiencing Inner Stillness and Silence

- Learn the difference between stillness and resting in stillness.
- Rest to allow yourself to relax, recover, and feel refreshed.
- Listen for God's voice when you are relaxed.
- Create quiet environments to help foster stillness; over time, this will not be necessary.
- Allow yourself to sink into your prayers and Scripture.

CHAPTER 9

Pain, Pain, Go Away

Allowing for God's Healing to Enter Our Minds and Bodies

- Recognize that pain is the body's way of letting you know it needs more care and attention than it's currently receiving.
- Understand that somatization—"the body keeps score"—often means your emotional distress is making your body sick.
- Heal within the parasympathetic nervous system.

- Breathe to impact physical pain by bringing focused pain relief and more oxygen to tissues that need healing.
- Notice how the way you breathe can influence the way you feel your emotions, either in the moment or after the fact.

CHAPTER 10

Sacred Heart of Jesus

Accessing the Heart Physically and Spiritually

- Learn to tune in to the physical heartbeat.
- Do the same exercise while doing IBF. It can be easier to experience the heartbeat when you're holding your breath.
- Meditate on heart expansion.
- Meditate on forgiveness.
- Meditate on healing.
- Experience the heart of Jesus: "Beat in me, O Heart of Jesus."

CHAPTER 11

The Return of the Two Sons

Experiencing Our Father's Love

- Experience unconditional love to love unconditionally.

- Understand the love the father had for each of his sons.
- Be aware of the older and younger son within yourself.
- Run back into your Father's arms with no hesitation to rest, have your wounds tended to, and experience healing.
- Use breath to remember God's love for you.

CHAPTER 12

Love for Our Father

Encountering the Eucharist with Love

- Take the opportunity with every breath to
  - connect with your heart and with God who abides within you
  - love God and to love others
  - pray unceasingly
  - become aware of mental and physical blockages to allow God into all areas of your life
  - surrender to God
  - allow God to sit in the driver's seat
  - be prepared and vigilant when He appears
  - remember your identity as a child of God
  - keep the door of your heart unlocked

Our God is a God of surprises.

—POPE FRANCIS

Conclusion

- Experience breath as the smallest act we can do with great love, following Saint Thérèse's "little way" and borrowing a line from Mother Teresa of Calcutta.
- Access our hearts through breath, for that is where God abides.
- Embrace each breath as another opportunity to love.
- Recognize the power of our breath in hearing God's voice and experiencing God's peace.

Remember that nothing is small in the eyes of God.
Do all that you do with love.

—SAINT THÉRÈSE OF LISIEUX

Additional Prayers

Here are some additional prayers to help you practice your breath work. Use the slashes as a guide for where to pause. Choose a count that comes very easily to you so that the prayer can be said naturally.

Radiating Christ

Dear Jesus, / help us to spread Your fragrance wherever we go; / flood our souls with Your spirit and life. / Penetrate and possess our whole beings so utterly, / that our lives may only be a radiance of Yours. / Shine through us, and be so in us / that every soul we come in contact with / may feel Your presence in our souls. / Let them look up and see no longer us, / but only Jesus! / Stay with us / and then we shall begin to shine / as You shine, / so to shine / as to be a light to others. / The light, O Jesus, / will be all from You; / none of it will be ours. / It will be You, shining on others through us. / Let us thus praise You / the way You love best, / by shining on those around us. / Let us preach You without preaching, / not by words but by our example, / by the catching force, / the sympathetic influence of what we do, / the evident fullness of the love / our hearts bear to You. / Amen.

Anima Christi

Soul of Christ, sanctify me. / Body of Christ, save me. / Blood of Christ, inebriate me. / Water from the side of Christ, wash me. / Passion of Christ, strengthen me. / O good Jesus, hear me. / Within Thy wounds hide me. / Suffer me not to be separated from Thee. / From the malicious enemy defend me. / In the hour of my death call me and bid me come to Thee. / That with Thy saints, I may praise Thee / forever and ever. / Amen.

Magnificat

My soul proclaims the greatness of the Lord. / My spirit rejoices in God my savior. / For He has looked upon His handmaid's lowliness; / behold, from now on will all ages call me blessed. / The mighty one has done great things for me / and holy is His name. / His mercy is from age to age / to those who fear Him. / He has shown might with His arm, / dispersed the arrogant of mind and heart. / He has thrown down the rulers from their thrones / but lifted up the lowly. / The hungry He has filled with good things;

/ the rich He has sent away empty. / He has helped Israel His servant, / remembering His mercy / according to His promise to our fathers, / to Abraham and to his descendants forever.

Prayer to Begin Each Day

As morning breaks, I think of You, O Lord, / and my desire to serve You joyfully. / With gladness, I consecrate this day to Your Sacred Heart / and offer whatever joys and sacrifices come my way. / Thank You for the graces You will send, / all the love, all the beauty, and the ways You will answer my prayers. / Today may I love my enemies and treat others as I would ask to be treated; / may I forgive seventy times seven and show mercy; / may I welcome the prodigal son, have compassion for the Samaritan; / be a peacemaker and love my neighbor unconditionally. / Take all my heart and mind and strength, O Lord, / that this day may be truly lived for Your greater honor and glory / and for the salvation of souls. / Amen.

Prayer After Holy Communion

Lord Jesus, I welcome You into my body and my soul. / Let me receive You with joy and fidelity, in imitation of Saint Joseph. / Enter into my heart and my affections, my work and my rest, / my thoughts and my feelings, my mind and my distractions, / my strengths and my weaknesses, my words and my actions, / my family and my relationships, my hopes and my fears, / my plans and my disappointments, my successes and my failures, / my wounds and my attempts at forgiveness, my past memories and this present moment, / my desires and my striving for holiness, my prayers and my devotion. / Guide me by Your Holy Spirit to faithfully carry out all that You ask of me. / Give me strength and grace to always embrace Your will, / that I may share in the peace that Saint Joseph experienced / as he lovingly held You in his arms and pressed You close to his heart. / Amen.

Take, Lord, Receive

Take, Lord, receive all my liberty, / my memory, my understanding, and my entire will. / All that I have and possess, You, Lord, have given to me. / I now give it back to You, O Lord. All of it is Yours. / Dispose of it according to Your will. / Give me only Your love and Your grace, for that is enough for me.

Prayer to Your Guardian Angel

Angel sent by God to guide me, / be my light and walk beside me; / be my guardian and protect me; / on the paths of life direct me. / Amen.

Prayer of Surrender

Lord, I pray for the poverty of spirit to hear Your voice, / for wisdom to understand Your Word, / for faith to believe Your Word, / for humility to obey Your Word. / Lord, please grant me the knowledge to go deeper into the mysteries of the kingdom of heaven, / the grace to submit myself to You in childlike abandon. / Keep me as the apple of Your eye. / Hide me in the shadow of Your wings. / Lord, let me see Your face, / and when I am awake, let me be filled with Your presence. / Never let me sin with my tongue, / and fill me with courage to bring You to others. / Lord, grace me to love You more and more / with every passing moment till the end of time. / In Jesus's name, / amen.

In the silence of the heart, God speaks.

—SAINT TERESA OF CALCUTTA

Acknowledgments

For the work you have read, I did not have a specific teacher who combined science and faith. Jesus and the Holy Spirit have been my main teachers. I would, however, like to highlight four teachers—Wim Hof, Dr. Buteyko, Patrick McKeown, and Shane Heins—who helped me understand breath, the cold, and movement in scientific ways. I would like to especially mention Wim Hof, whose infectious passion made me aware of the role breath plays in matters of love and healing, and what a unifying force it is.

A teacher is not a teacher without students. My first students in the topics described in this book were the Sisters of the Missionaries of Charity in Phoenix, Arizona. The transformation I saw in them as they practiced the exercises I shared, alongside their belief in the work that I was doing, provided me with the encouragement I needed during moments of doubt and apprehension while writing this book. I eventually gave a conference to the Sisters in Memphis, Tennessee, before I decided the book was ready to be published.

I also want to thank my friends in Houston, Texas, and

other parts of the world who closely watched me walk this journey. In a special way, I want to thank Christopher Shannon and James (Jim) T. Hackett. Chris walked with me through my journey of becoming a breath coach and going through a religious conversion, and Jim has been a great inspiration to me and was the first person to read the book after its completion. His kind words of encouragement gave me the affirmation I needed to make this book a reality. I thank them both from the bottom of my heart.

In addition to the various priests, religious brothers and sisters, and spiritual companions who encouraged me to put this work down on paper, I would like to thank five priests in particular: Fr. Marty Lott, OP, my spiritual director, who guided me to keep teaching even if people around me didn't understand the work I was doing. Fr. Jilson Panakkal, who was the first priest to invite me to give a talk on breath at his parish. It was his parishioners who pushed me to put this work down on paper. Fr. Mariusz Wirkowski, who was the first priest to go through the exercises himself and encouraged me to get the book published. Fr. Andreas Kramarz, LC, who brought this book to completion through his in-depth editing and who wrote a foreword for it. Finally, Fr. Brian Kolodiejchuk, MC, for introducing me to my agent, Claudia Cross, without whom this book would not have been published. I thank them all for their belief in the Holy Spirit guiding me to do this work and for their consistent support along the way.

Last but not least, I would like to thank the communion of saints who walked with me through the journey of putting the contents of this book together. Specifically, I would like to thank Saint Teresa of Calcutta, who is my Confirmation saint. She inspires me to offer every breath for the love of God. I would also like to thank Saint Paul, for encouraging me to pray unceasingly; Saint Teresa of Avila, for modeling the path of pursuing self-knowledge; Saint Ignatius of Loyola, for emphasizing the importance of silence in our prayer life and conscious self-examination; Saint Faustina, for sharing her experience of the love and mercy of God; Saint Blaise, for revealing the healing effects associated with breathing correctly; Saint Thérèse of Lisieux, for giving me the title of this book; Saint John the Baptist, for showing us how to decrease in order for the Lord to increase within us; Saint Teresa Benedicta of the Cross, for showing us that it is possible to love carrying our cross; and Saint Joseph the Worker, for recognizing that the work we put into every breath can lead to a sanctifying life.

During the course of writing this book, I became a Benedictine oblate (ObSB) at the Monastery of Christ in the Desert in New Mexico. I praise God for guiding me from time to time into the desert, where silence continues to be an essential part of my life.

Many of the insights I have shared here were discovered during my study of the breathing techniques in which I am certified, my journey of self-exploration, and the grace I received from God. It has made me appreciate the roles that both science and faith play in our lives. Ultimately, the journey always begins with childlike curiosity. Since God is infinite, there are an infinite number of ways to seek Him within us. This book describes just one of the many ways that may be worth pursuing.

> I pray that the God of our Lord Jesus Christ, the Father of glory, may give you a spirit of wisdom and revelation as you come to know him, so that, with the eyes of your heart enlightened, you may know what is the hope to which he has called you, what are the riches of his glorious inheritance among the saints, and what is the immeasurable greatness of his power for us who believe, according to the working of his great power. (Ephesians 1:17–19)

To God be all the glory.

ABOUT THE AUTHOR

Shereen Yusuff, who converted from Islam, has embraced the Catholic Church and is now a Benedictine oblate. A certified breath and movement coach, she has spent years exploring the intimate connection between breath, the heart, and prayer. An accomplished endurance athlete, Shereen has completed marathons, ultramarathons, and Ironman triathlons. With a background in engineering and over two decades in both the private and public sectors, she brings a unique integration of scientific insight, athletic discipline, and spiritual depth to her work.

Through her Suda Prem Studio and her service to multiple religious communities, Shereen has guided others to encounter God more deeply by overcoming the inner roadblocks that keep them from true joy. She now shares the fruits of this journey in *Seeking the Spirit Within.* To learn more about her work, please visit www.Suda-Prem.com.